Building Touch Interfaces with HTML5

Speed up your site and create amazing user experiences

DEVELOP AND DESIGN

Stephen Woods

PEACHPIT PRESS
WWW.PEACHPIT.COM

Building Touch Interfaces with HTML5: Develop and Design

Stephen Woods

Peachpit Press

www.peachpit.com

To report errors, please send a note to errata@peachpit.com.
Peachpit Press is a division of Pearson Education.

Copyright © 2013 by Stephen Woods

Project Editor: Nancy Peterson
Production Editor: Rebecca Chapman-Winter
Development Editor: Jeff Riley
Compositor: Danielle Foster
Technical Editor: Nicholas C. Zakas
Copyeditor: Gretchen Dykstra
Proofer: Darren Meiss
Indexer: Jack Lewis
Cover Design: Aren Straiger
Interior Design: Mimi Heft

ISBN 13: 978-0-321-88765-8
ISBN 10:   0-321-88765-4

Printed and bound in the United States of America

9 8 7 6 5 4 3 2 1

To Sashimi, the best cat ever.

ACKNOWLEDGEMENTS

Thanks to Jeff Riley, Nancy Peterson, Michael Nolan, and the staff at Peachpit for making the book possible and my words less incoherent. Thanks to Nicholas Zakas for his exceptionally detailed and thoughtful criticism about this book and for his mentorship at Yahoo!

Thanks as well to Stoyan Stefanov for his last-minute review and invaluable experience in the world of technical writing. Thanks also to Guy Podjarny for his time and research.

This book wouldn't have been possible without the support of my manager, Ross Harmes, as well as the rest of the front-end team at Flickr.

Thanks to Benjamin for showing me the many uses for mobile devices.

Finally, thank you to Elise for putting up with me while I spent hours every evening staring at my computer and a pile of cell phones.

ABOUT THE AUTHOR

Stephen Woods is a Senior Front-end Engineer at Flickr. He has been developing user interfaces for the web since the end of the last century. He has worked at Yahoo! since 2006. Before Flickr, he developed JavaScript platforms that supported the Yahoo! home page and worked on the UI team at Yahoo! Personals. He's an expert with the full web stack, but his primary interest is making responsive user interfaces with web technologies. Stephen has spoken at SXSW and HTML5DevConf about touch interfaces and he has been published in *.net* magazine.

CONTENTS

INTRODUCTION

As of this writing, 11.42 percent of web visits are via a mobile device (according to Stat-Counter.com). One year ago that was 7 percent. Three years ago it was 1.77 percent. Desktops will be with us for a while, but the future of the web will be on mobile devices.

For web developers, supporting mobile devices is the biggest change since the web standards revolution of the early 2000s. Mobile devices all have HTML5-capable, thoroughly modern browsers. They have limited memory and slow CPUs. They often connect via high-latency connections. Most importantly, they all have touch interfaces.

Developing for mobile is developing for touch. Many of the skills you use for desktop web development carry over to the mobile web, but some things are quite different—and getting those things right can be difficult. I wrote this book to help you get the new things right.

WHO THIS BOOK IS FOR

This book was written for two types of readers:

- Experienced web developers who have never developed for mobile or touch interfaces and want to learn how.
- Developers who've been working in mobile but have struggled to make their mobile websites feel right.

This book is not for absolute beginners. You'll need to have a working knowledge of the web front-end: HTML, CSS, and JavaScript. Prior experience with the new APIs and features of HTML5 and CSS3 won't hurt either.

Most importantly, this book is for people who aren't content with a mobile site that's just good enough. If you want to build a site that feels fast and smooth, this book is for you.

WHAT YOU WILL LEARN

This book is focused on making touch interfaces that feel fast. It's structured in roughly the same way I approach optimizing a website. The first half covers what I consider the basics—concepts that make any website faster, but mobile sites in particular. Chapters 2 and 3 show you how to build a simple site and make it load faster. Chapter 4 helps you speed up users' next visit to the site with caching. Chapter 5 is all about removing page loads all together and structuring applications to maximize real and perceived performance.

The second half of the book is specifically about touch interfaces, in particular making them feel as smooth and fast as possible. The book gets more complex as it goes on. If you feel like the later chapters are over your head, try applying what you've learned so far in your work and then coming back to some of the ideas I'll present toward the end. A website doesn't need pinch to zoom to be useful.

WHAT YOU'LL NEED

To get the most out of this book you'll need at least one touch-enabled device in addition to your computer. If you're only going to have one, I recommend an iOS 6 or Android 4 device. Having both is ideal if you can afford it.

When developing for the mobile web, try to get as many devices as possible. iOS and Android simulators are no substitute for real devices. When writing this book, I used a Samsung Galaxy S III with Android 4.0.4 (Ice Cream Sandwich), an iPhone 4, an iPhone 5, an iPad 1, and an HTC 8X (Windows 8). I supplemented these devices with the simulators.

At Flickr we have a similar set but we also have several Android tablets and a Kindle Fire.

FRAMEWORKS

This book doesn't use jQuery or any other JavaScript framework. You'll learn about a few specialized libraries, but we'll focus as much as possible on native DOM APIs. That's not to say you should avoid frameworks—far from it! But I want to make sure you understand how things really work. When you decide to build a site with jQuery mobile, Backbone.js, Zepto.js, or any other framework, you'll be much more comfortable understanding what's really going on.

The other huge benefit to understanding the native DOM APIs is that when you find a bug or a problem in a library you can patch it yourself and make a pull request with your fixes, benefiting the entire community. Appendix A lists some handy debugging tools.

Appendix B lists a few of the more common mobile-focused frameworks. When you build a new site, I recommend carefully evaluating your needs, including as little library code as you can, and adding only what you need.

The appendices are not printed in the book. They can be found at the book's companion website: touch-interfaces.com

THE WEBSITE

All the code samples in this book as well as late-breaking changes can be found at the companion website: touch-interfaces.com. The code samples are also mirrored on GitHub, where you can file issues with the samples and submit pull requests: https://github.com/saw/touch-interfaces.

WELCOME TO THE MOBILE WEB

Websites are built with HTML, CSS, and JavaScript. Mobile websites are no different. All you really need to get started is a web browser and a text editor, but to be
really productive I recommend a few more tools.

THE TOOLCHAIN

The easiest process is to develop with a text editor and a desktop browser,
then keep a touch device around for testing.

A TEXT EDITOR & A WEBKIT BROWSER

I use TextMate 2 (github. com/textmate/textmate) for MacOS X, but any edi-tor will do.

Because the vast majority of mobile devices run a WebKit browser, you will find that Chrome or Safari is a an essential tool to being productive. It isn't the same as testing on the real device but it's a lot easier and essential.

A WEB SERVER

In order to test your site on an actual device you will need to serve pages on your local wireless net-work. On the Mac I find MAMP (www.mamp.info) to be a very convenient tool for this, but using the built-in Apache web server will work as well.

A TOUCH DEVICE

There is no substitute for a physical device. If you can afford it, I recom-mend having at least a recent Android phone and an iOS device. If you can only afford one phone it's helpful to find people who will let you borrow their phones for a moment to test on.

TESTING ACROSS DEVICES

You can't assume that all WebKit browsers are created equal. You should test your app in iOS 5, iOS 6, Android 2.3, Android 4.0, Android 4.1 (Chrome), and IE 10. Here is a guide to how to test on these devices, even if you don't have access to the device itself.

IOS SAFARI

Apple provides a quite capable simulator with XCode. The simulator can run as iOS 5 or 6 and as a tablet or phone. It also supports remote debugging with Safari. It really is a great tool and assuming you have a Mac this is a critical part of your toolset. XCode is available for free from the Mac App store.

ANDROID

Google provides emulators for just about every version of Android. These are available with the Android SDK (developer. android.com/sdk). Once you have the Android SDK, images for various Android versions are separate downloads. Keep in mind these are the official builds from Google; Android versions on actual devices can vary quite a bit.

WINDOWS 8

Microsoft does provide an emulator for Windows Phone 8; it's available with the SDK (dev. windowsphone.com/ en-us/downloadsdk). The emulator runs only on Windows. IE 10 for the desktop is the same browser, so most debugging can be down with the desktop browser rather than the emulator.

DEBUGGING

Debugging websites on phones can be a chore, but there are a lot of tools available to make it easier. I've provided a list of several on the website in Appendix A.

THE DIFFERENCE BETWEEN A TOUCH DEVICE AND A DESKTOP

The vast majority of touch devices in the world are mobile devices. On the desktop developers are mostly worried about making their sites work on different browsers. Understanding the details of browser differences is a big part of a web developer's job.

On mobile the problem isn't browsers, it's devices. Sure, there are a few different browsers on mobile, and there are some differences between them, but in general mobile browsers are as capable as their desktop counterparts. There are four major considerations that separate mobile devices from desktops:

- Form factors
- Lack of computing horsepower
- How people use them
- Touch interface

FORM FACTORS

The most obvious difference between a mobile device and a desktop (or laptop) computer is the size. Mobile devices are small and they have small screens. They don't have mice or, in most cases, keyboards.

Touch devices currently come in three main form factors: phones, small tablets, and large tablets. Large tablets include the (non-mini) iPads and the various 10-inch Android tablets, like the Nexus 10. Small tablet screens are generally around 7 inches diagonal and include the Nexus 7, Galaxy Note, and iPad Mini.

The browsers on all of these devices are full screen, all the time. The only way a user can "resize" the browser is by rotating the device between landscape and portrait mode. Optimizing for mobile isn't a matter of making it fit one size, but making sure your site fits in all the sizes a mobile devices comes in.

MOBILE DEVICES ARE UNDERPOWERED

As of this writing the most powerful touch device available is the fourth generation iPad. It is, by all accounts, an incredibly powerful machine. Based on benchmarks it's about as powerful as a Power Mac G5—the last generation of Motorola Macintoshes, released in 2004.

It's safe to say that most users aren't using the latest and greatest device. The "free with contract" phones available from most providers, like the iPhone 4 and the Samsung Galaxy Exhilarate, are much slower. These phones are comparable in CPU power to the fastest desktop PCs available around the turn of the century. The Apple iPhone 3GS, still widely used, has 256 MB RAM, one core, and CPU performance roughly equivalent to the last generation of iMacs sold with CRT screens. Although the capabilities of mobile devices will continue to grow, they are still quite slow compared to the average desktop. Their saving grace is the fact that most of the recent ones have separate GPUs. An iPhone 4 can be thought of as a crappy computer with a powerful graphics card.

PEOPLE USE TOUCH DEVICES DIFFERENTLY

People use mobile differently than desktops. Using a desktop computer is a specific task; you're probably not doing much else when you're using your computer. Mobile devices, both phones and tablets, are usually something people use in small bursts while they're doing something else. They might be riding a bus, waiting in a line, or just sitting in a boring meeting.

Say, for example, you were creating a financial news site. On the desktop a user might click around for a while and then spend several minutes reading an article. A mobile user might come with one specific task to accomplish and only a few seconds to do it. Desktop sites shouldn't be slow, but a desktop user will give you more time before getting frustrated. If your site takes a little too long to load, the user can change tabs to look at something else and then come back. On mobile, the user won't give you that chance.

MOBILE DEVICES ARE TOUCH DEVICES

All the new smartphones and tablets on the market share one very important characteristic: they all have touch interfaces—in most cases, multi-touch interfaces. The convenient form factors, beautiful screens, and advanced features are minor advantages compared to the revolutionary possibilities of using a touch screen.

DEVICES IN THE WILD

When the iPhone arrived in 2007 there was no other smartphone with a "real" touch-aware web browser. There also was no device available to consumers with a multi-touch interface. Most other smartphones used a stylus for interaction, as did the few tablets that existed at the time. Today there are hundreds of touch devices in circulation. It's impossible to keep track of each new device, but they can generally be categorized by their operating systems, form factors, and available web browsers.

OPERATING SYSTEMS

There are four major operating systems for touch devices on the market today:

- iOS
- Android
- Blackberry OS
- Windows 8

Android is by far the most popular on phones. According to International Data Corporation (IDC), 75 percent of smartphones shipped in the third quarter of 2012 were running Android. 14.9 percent were running iOS. Other operating systems had only single-digit share. (This does not include Windows Phone 8, which wasn't released until October 2012.)

IOS

iOS is the operating system running on all phones and tablets from Apple. Because Apple controls the hardware, all iPads and iPhones work the same way, varying only in size and power. Apple also pushes out software updates without going through carriers, meaning that Apple devices are much more likely to be using the latest version of the OS. David Smith, an iOS developer, found that 79.2 percent of users of his app were using iOS 6 or greater (as of December 2012) and 94 percent were using 5.1 or greater.

NOTE: David Smith keeps these stats up to date on his website at david-smith.org/iosversionstats/.

Apple upgrades the browser with the OS and does not allow the user to install a different browser engine. At least for now it is reasonable to expect users to have nothing older than one major version back of iOS and iOS Safari.

ANDROID

Android is in a very different situation. Android is open source with phone manufacturers free to customize it as they see fit, so the actual user interface varies a lot between phones.

There are three major versions of Android: 2, 3, and 4. Android 3 (Honeycomb) is a tablet-only OS. About 50 percent of Android phones are running version 2.3.x (Gingerbread). The latest version, Android 4.1 (Jelly Bean) is not widely installed, with less than 10 percent of devices running it as of January 2013, but that number is growing quickly. The current crop of "flagship" phones, like the Samsung Galaxy SIII, are still shipping with Android 4.0.x (Ice Cream Sandwich). Android 4.1 supports both tablets and phones.

NOTE: Google provides these statistics at developer.android.com/about/dashboards/.

Android includes a default browser but also lets users install different browsers. Since version 4.1, the default browser on Android has been Chrome.

KINDLE FIRE

The Amazon Kindle Fire runs a highly customized version of Android that doesn't include any of the native Android apps and has its own browser called Silk. The Silk browser is notable for its ability to run on the client device or on Amazon's cloud. This can dramatically improve performance, particularly on high-latency connections. There are a few implications for developers, which are covered in Chapter 4, "Speeding Up the Next Visit."

BLACKBERRY OS

The Blackberry was the first really successful smartphone. As of December 2012 its market share was rapidly dwindling: only about 4.3 percent of devices run this operating system. Blackberry also sells a tablet, called the Playbook. Both devices use the same WebKit-based web browser. There's also a long tail of legacy non-touch Blackberry devices.

WINDOWS

Windows Phone 8 includes Microsoft's first fully touch-enabled browser. The phone comes with Internet Explorer 10 built in, as well as the ability to create apps that run in a "tile" with an HTML5 runtime.

DEVICES AND FORM FACTORS

The most notable difference between desktops and mobile devices is their form factor. Mobile devices come in two primary form factors: phones and tablets.

PHONES

The most common touch devices are smartphones. With very few exceptions, they all have the same basic form factor: rectangles with portrait touchscreens. The most important thing to consider when developing for phones is their small screen size. Interactive elements need to be large enough to be manipulated by a finger; content should fit on the small screen.

TABLETS

Tablets are a much more diverse category. They vary from the tiny Galaxy Note (5.3-inch screen) to the 13-inch Windows "convertible" tablets arriving on the market. Some tablets, like the iPad, are normally used in portrait orientation. Others are intended to be used in landscape mode. Just like phones, all of these tablets have browsers that fill their screens.

Despite this diversity, the actual tablets in use are quite homogenous: iPads outsell all the competition by a healthy margin. The only other manufacturer with a double-digit share is Samsung. The most popular form factors are 10-inch (like the iPad) and 7-inch (like the iPad Mini and Kindle Fire).

HARDWARE GRAPHICS ACCELERATION

As mentioned before, an iPhone can be thought of as a crappy computer with a decent video card. Just as the CPU and memory available varies from device to device, so does the graphics hardware. Prior to Android 3, the browser has no accelerated compositing at all. That means that no matter how smooth an animation might be on an iPhone 5, it will never be as smooth on an older phone running Android 2.3.3.

All current mobile devices use what is called "shared memory" for graphics. Unlike a graphics card on a desktop computer, the graphics on a mobile device don't have dedicated memory; they have to share the system memory. That means that as more things are added to graphics memory, less memory is available to the system. This will be important to keep in mind when we discuss accelerated graphics later on.

BROWSERS

Mercifully, the browser picture is much less complex than the device picture. WebKit is far and away the most popular mobile browser, powering the default browser in all Apple, Android, and Blackberry devices. Windows Phones run IE 10. The most popular alternative mobile browser is Opera Mobile, with less than 1% of market share.

WEBKIT

WebKit started the engine for an open source browser called Konqueror. Apple developed this engine into WebKit, the browser engine behind Safari. WebKit was always a very capable browser and it was part of what made the first iPhone great. Until Android 4.1, a WebKit-based browser generally called "Android Browser" was installed on Android devices. As of 4.1 "Android Browser" has been replaced by Chrome for Android, also a WebKit browser.

WebKit browsers are similar, but not identical. Their rendering behavior is very nearly identical across implementations, with some small variations, but the feature support does vary quite a bit. I'll note the differences when they crop up.

IOS SAFARI

The iOS version of WebKit is the only browser engine allowed on iOS. It is usually accessed via the Safari browser, but it's also accessible from native apps with the Cocoa UIWebView class.

ANDROID BROWSER

Android Browser, which inside Android is just called "browser," is the built-in browser for Android. It is based on WebKit, but it is not Chrome. The capabilities of the Android browser vary across versions. Surprisingly the browser doesn't necessarily have more features in later versions. The Android 2.3.3 browser is in some ways more full featured than the one in 4.0.1. I'll note the differences later on.

CHROME FOR ANDROID

Chrome for Android is usually about one release behind the Chrome stable branch. As of Android 4.1 the native Android Browser has been replaced with Chrome.

IE10 FOR WINDOWS

IE10, unlike all previous versions of Internet Explorer, has feature parity or near-parity with WebKit. IE10 has a very different API for touch events, but the features are the same.

THE REST

There are many other browsers. The most popular are Opera Mobile and Firefox mobile, both available for Android. Both browsers are very capable and implement roughly the same features as WebKit. Where the syntax varies I will try to note it.

HTML5

One thing that all the mobile browsers share is support for the advanced browser features generally called HTML5. But what exactly is HTML5?

HTML5 technically refers to the markup language and set of APIs specified by the Web Hypertext Application Technology Working Group (WHATWG). It is designed to succeed HTML4 by defining features that meet the needs of web applications which, when HTML5 was first proposed, had outgrown the original document-centric model of HTML.

In practice, HTML5 has become a byword for a suite of standardized and emerging technologies that dramatically expand the traditional "web stack" (HTML, CSS, and JavaScript).

THE SPEC

Unlike previous HTML specifications, the WHATWG has decided not to define official versions. Instead HTML5 (now officially renamed just "HTML") is a living standard, allowing new APIs and features to be added on an ad-hoc basis. The World Wide Web Consortium (W3C) is working to create an official, versioned specification.

Because HTML5 is a living standard, browser makers are adding new features before standardization. This means that the total set of features is similar across browsers, but the specific features available in browsers and their implementation varies.

Knowing what makes it into the specification is useful, but for now developers need to know what browsers have what features, and how to handle them. In this book I'll note which features are part standardized, and which features are emerging.

> **NOTE:** The HTML5 "living standard" is available at www.whatwg.org. You can read the complete official W3C spec at w3.org.

THE SUITE

The power of what is generally called HTML5 comes from the broader suite of technologies. CSS3 (and nonspecified CSS features from browser makers) gives us the ability to create dynamic and beautiful interfaces without sacrificing responsiveness.

In this book I'm considering HTML5 as the broader suite. Unfortunately, today just "sticking to the spec" won't give us the tools we need to create great touch interfaces. In the future I expect more standardization on the features and more emerging APIs. The exciting thing about the web, including the mobile web, is that it's always changing, and we as developers must change with it.

THE UNCANNY VALLEY: WHAT MAKES A TOUCH INTERFACE RESPONSIVE?

I have a two-and-a-half-year-old son. He's been able to unlock an iPad and find the app he's looking for since he was one. He was able to unlock the iPad before he could talk. I've compared notes with other parents, and my son isn't precocious. Touch interfaces just make intuitive sense to kids: touching and moving things is one of the most basic things humans do. Touch interfaces are very intuitive and powerful. But they can easily feel broken.

There's a theory in robotics called "the uncanny valley": the more a robot looks like a person, the more appealing it is to us, but when a robot starts to look very similar to a human, but not exactly, we find it weird and creepy. The "valley" refers to the dip in our comfort level with the robot's human likeness.

A touch interface feels very natural—it feels like moving real objects around. When things aren't right it doesn't feel slow, it feels broken. The interface stops feeling natural when the illusion of direct manipulation is broken. That feeling of brokenness comes from falling into the uncanny valley; instead of feeling natural, it feels weird.

CHIEF O'BRIEN AND DIRECT MANIPULATION

Like a lot of people in my generation, my first introduction to touch interfaces was through *Star Trek: The Next Generation.* If you haven't seen it, all the control panels on the ship were touch screens: actually multi-touch interfaces. Apparently the reason for this was purely one of budget. The creators of the show wanted sets that showed a lot of complexity in all the control panels, but they couldn't afford to build the sets on the budget of a syndicated show. So they came up with the idea of printing the interface onto transparencies with lights behind them to create the appearance of touch screens.

Chief O'Brien, the guy who operated the transporter, used a three-finger swipe gesture to energize the transporter. I think that gesture is really interesting. The interface had three sliders; the actor naturally thought to touch and drag the sliders as if they were physical objects. That's the way people expect to use a touch interface. Because they're touching the screen, they intuitively feel that it should move like a real object when they interact with it.

The Apple Touch Interface Guidelines call this concept "direct manipulation." Rather than using a control to make something happen, a touch interface should ideally give the user the impression that he is directly manipulating the thing he is interacting with.

You'll notice that as Chief O'Brien moves his fingers, little indicators move with them. This is partly to keep up the illusion of direct manipulation. But it's also providing feedback that the computer is registering his interaction.

USER FEEDBACK

I like to think that an interface that feels fast doesn't have to be fast. It just has to be responsive—it responds immediately to the user to let him know that something happened. My favorite example is TiVo. Not the HD version I have under my TV today, but the original TiVo box that shipped in 1999. That box had a 54 MHz CPU and only 16 MB of RAM. Although TiVo had special hardware for encoding and decoding video, it could take quite a while from when a user clicked on a show to when the box actually started playing. There were lots of complaints about TiVo, but nobody ever complained that it was slow. That's because of the familiar TiVo beep-boop sound.

When the user clicked on a show, he heard the sound immediately. I don't know how much engineering time went into making sure that the sound was so immediate, but it made all the difference. That sound let the user know right away that his request had been heard.

On a web interface, this kind of immediate feedback is just as important. On desktop websites, most interactions are discrete: one click and something happens. On a touch interface, many interactions aren't discrete: they're continuous because they're gestures. When a user is gesturing on a screen you can't wait until the gesture is done for feedback, because as far as the user knows the gesture isn't even working!

Consider swiping. Swiping is moving a finger across the screen to perform some action. Ideally as the user swipes, the interface element should move with the swiping. If swiping is used to move between pages, the whole page should move with your finger. If the interface didn't move, you'd have no way of knowing that something was happening until the end. A swipe gesture with no feedback would be like a keyboard that didn't show anything until you finished typing a word. Feedback for a gesture can't wait until the end. For the interface to feel responsive, the feedback must also be continuous: if the user's finger is moving, the interface needs to be moving as well.

The corollary to this is that the interface must in fact *always* be moving if the user is gesturing, even if the user reaches the end of a gesture. When the interface stops moving during a gesture, it feels like it died.

For example, if you were to create a slide show where the user could swipe between slides, when the user reached the end of the slides you wouldn't want the gesture to stop working: to the user that would feel like the interface died. Instead let the user keep swiping, but when she lets go, snap the previous slide into position. The user gets feedback that her gesture was heard, there just aren't any more slides. That's why Apple relies so heavily on elements "snapping back" into place at the end of a gesture. It's really the only way to show a user that he's reached the bottom of something without breaking the metaphor.

CONVENTIONS

Every user interface has conventions. On the desktop there are windows, buttons, scroll boxes, close boxes. On mobile there is a new set of conventions. By being the first mover, Apple managed to create both sets of UI conventions.

You don't need to have everything exactly the same as a native iOS app. But knowing what gestures and elements mean in a mobile context is important: don't use a swipe gesture to select something when the native apps use it to mean delete. Don't override gestures that are normally reserved for the OS (like tap and hold for context menus, pinch to zoom, double-tap to zoom) unless you're re-implementing the same basic behavior. (You'll learn more about this in Chapter 10, "Scrolling and Swiping" and Chapter 11, "Pinching and Other Complex Gestures.")

WRAPPING UP

The touch landscape is constantly changing, but for the most part the differences between web browsers are small. The differences in performance are bigger, but it's possible to make a great user interface on touch devices with just HTML5.

Because of the nature of touch devices, fast is critical. User feedback is the most important part of making things seem fast.

CHAPTER 2

Creating a Simple Content Site

Content sites make up a large portion of the Internet. After all, the Web was created for consuming text, and a lot of what people still do there is reading text on a web page. Although making a content site responsive on a touch device is very important, many content sites aren't particularly responsive.

In this chapter we'll build a website about birds in California for our client, the Awesome Bird Foundation. Because people don't generally do much bird watching at home, our goal for the site will be to make it usable on mobile and the desktop. The client has visions of millions of articles being linked from Twitter so users can click through and read some great bird content. We don't want those readers tapping away before the site loads. Every millisecond counts. After optimizing everything on the server, we still want the site to load as quickly as possible.

Obviously the site will load more slowly on a high-latency 3G connection than it will on a 100 MB office connection. But once the bytes start coming, it's essential to draw them immediately. To do that we'll start with the basics: the Document Object Model (DOM) and the Cascading Style Sheets (CSS).

The designer has given us two mock-ups: a desktop version (**Figure 2.1**) and a mobile version (**Figure 2.2**).

FIGURE 2.1 A desktop view of Birds of California.

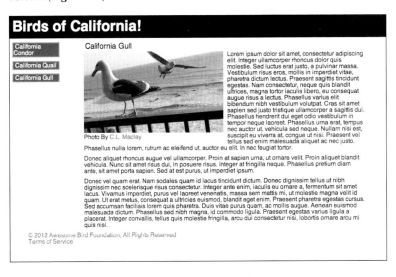

FIGURE 2.2 A mobile view of Birds of California. *(Photo © 2011 C. L. Maclay made available under a Creative Commons Attribution 2.0 License)*

Looking at these mock-ups, it's clear that this won't be too difficult. But don't forget that the website has to work on both mobile and desktop devices. As developers, we like to write as little code as possible, because we know that everything we write, we'll need to maintain. At the same time, we want the site experience to be the best it can be on any screen.

Ideally we could write the code once and use it on all devices. In many cases we can take advantage of the new media queries in CSS 3 to avoid forking at all. As discussed in

Chapter 1, "The Touch Landscape," mobile devices are very limited compared to desktops. The beautiful, complex interaction that works great on the desktop might choke and die on less capable mobile devices. You really have to approach each case separately. But as a general rule, simple content sites should be able to run more or less the same code on desktop and mobile. The Birds of California site is a perfect candidate.

CHOOSING A PHILOSOPHY: MOBILE FIRST OR MOBILE LAST

The phrase "mobile first" refers to several trends in web development. It's a design philosophy, a development approach, and a way to structure CSS.

The design philosophy is simply the idea of creating a design that targets mobile devices, and then adapting it for the desktop. This isn't a design book, so I'll leave that to others more qualified (Luke Wroblewski's book *Mobile First* is a great start). The development approach is a similar idea: get the code working for mobile first, then adapt for desktop. Hypothetically this results in leaner code, which benefits desktop performance as well. In practice, a site with significant interactivity has to work so differently from the desktop site that there will be considerable code forking regardless. It's not a bad way to go, but I'm not convinced that it really saves any time.

True mobile-first CSS isn't quite ready for most production websites because Internet Explorer 8 doesn't support media queries. (We'll look more closely at media queries later in this chapter.) For this site we'll be using some HTML5 tags. That means to support IE properly, we'd need to do some extra work, or include a library like Modernizr. This book isn't about supporting IE, so I'm not going to cover this, but in production a site that works on mobile and desktop must support IE8.

CREATING THE MARKUP

For this site we'll do things "mobile last," but we'll use the same markup for both mobile and desktop. We'll focus on semantic markup, but because we're building this site to work on mobile devices, we'll also look at the DOM and CSS performance.

> **NOTE:** One of the downsides of "mobile last" is that mobile devices need to download (and parse) all the desktop styles. If you work "mobile first," then mobile devices can safely ignore styles that aren't needed. Again, this is a case-by-case issue.

When marking up a document, I divide it into regions that make sense semantically and that will also work well when styling the design. For the Birds of California site I put the navigation links inside a <nav> tag, inside an <aside> tag representing both the sidebar in the desktop design and the top navigation bar in the mobile design. For the content I created a <div> with the class main, which contains the photo, the title, and the copy.

The marked-up document is shown in **Listing 2.1**.

LISTING 2.1 Body markup

```
<body class="bd">
   <header class="container header">
      <h1>Birds of California!</h1>
   </header>

   <aside class="sidebar">
      <nav class="bird-nav">
         <ul class="bird-list">
            <!-- Redundant Class for performance -->
            <li class="nav-li">
               <a class="nav-link"
               → href="/california-condor">California Condor</a>
            </li>
            <li class="nav-li"><a class="nav-link"
            → href="/california-quail">California Quail</a></li>
            <li class="nav-li"><a class="nav-link"
            → href="/california-gull">California Gull</a></li>
         </ul>
      </nav>
   </aside>

   <div class="container main">
      <h2>California Gull</h2>
      <div class="hero-shot">
         <a href="http://www.flickr.com/photos/catlantis/5514922015/">
         <img class="hero-img" src="http://farm6.staticflickr.com/
         → 5171/5514922015_bfeab78ce0_z.jpg">
         </a>
         <p class="caption">Photo By <a href="http://www.flickr.com/photos/
         → catlantis/5514922015/">C.L.
      Maclay</a></p>
      </div>
      <section class="content">
```

```
      <p>Lorem ipsum dolor...</p>
    </section>

  </div>

  <footer class="container ft">
    <ul class="foot-links">
      <li><a href="/copyright">&copy; 2012 Awesome Bird Foundation,
        All Rights Reserved</a></li>
      <li><a href="/tos">Terms of Service</a></li>
    </ul>
  </footer>
</body>
```

You'll notice that there are quite a few classes that might seem redundant. For example, the navigation links are `<li>` tags with class "nav-li". There are two reasons for this:

1. Classes will be easier to manage as your codebase gets bigger. Using `nav-li` is clearer, less brittle, and easier to build on than a selector like "nav ul li".

2. Because the site will need to perform on the slowest free Android phone in the world, we need to be very picky when it comes to CSS selector performance—and that means avoiding descendent selectors.

Counter intuitively, when the browser parses a CSS selector it works from *right to left*. That means if it sees a rule like "nav ul li a" it first has to get all the elements that match a, then check that list to see if it matches li a and so on. Descendent selectors are the most expensive, even though they seem very convenient.

LAYING THE GROUNDWORK: THE <HEAD>

Listing 2.2 shows the <head> tag for the Birds of California site.

THE HTTP-EQUIV META PROPERTY

The http-equiv meta elements tell the browser to act as if the equivalent HTTP header was set. That lets you tell the browser things that the server normally would; this is particularly useful if you don't control the server. For example, if you'd like to set a cache header, but can't control the server, you can use the http-equiv property:

```
<meta http-equiv="expires" content="Wed, 05 August 2020 00:00:00 GMT">.
```

Be aware that server headers always take precedence, so you can only set or unset headers; you cannot override server headers.

LISTING 2.2 The `<head>` tag

```
<!DOCTYPE html>
<html>
<head>
    <meta charset="utf-8">
    <meta http-equiv="X-UA-Compatible" content="IE=edge,chrome=1">
    <meta name="viewport" content="width=device-width">
    <title>Birds of California</title>
    <link rel="stylesheet" href="reset.css" type="text/css"
media="screen" charset="utf-8">
    <link rel="stylesheet" href="birds.css" type="text/css" media="screen"
      charset="utf-8">
</head>
```

I started with an HTML5 doctype and specified the UTF-8 character set. It's important to specify a character set, not only to ensure the proper display of the document, but also to avoid possible security vulnerability with the UTF-7 character set. Normally the server will send a `Content-Type` header, but just in case I specify it in HTML as well.

I used an `http-equiv` property to set the nonstandard `"X-UA-Compatible"` header. The values are `chrome=1` and `IE=edge`, so that Chrome Frame would be used when available, and IE will render using the latest and best engine, rather than legacy mode.

The next meta property is called `viewport`. This is currently used only by touch devices, and it's very important to get it right.

UNDERSTANDING THE VIEWPORT

Before the iPhone, mobile browsers tried to adapt content to fit web pages, with varying success. iPhone Safari decided not to even try, and instead renders web pages on a virtual window of sorts, called the "viewport." Users can zoom in on portions of a web page, or zoom out to see the whole thing.

To give developers some sort of control over how the page is rendered, Apple provided the viewport meta element, which specifies how large the virtual window should be. This changes a lot of things about building web pages. Understanding the viewport is the beginning of building great mobile sites.

VIRTUAL PIXELS

As web developers we love pixels. Pixels are the most precise and simple way to lay out items on a web page. A pixel is the smallest thing on the screen; when we specify a pixel value we know exactly what that means. If you got out a microscope you could actually count those pixels on the screen.

The pixels you see on the screen on a mobile browser are not the same as the pixels on a desktop. That means that on an iPhone, you can't get out a microscope and verify that an element is 300px wide. An element with a width of 300px on a page without a viewport meta tag will be 300 virtual pixels wide on a viewport of the default width of 980px (**Figure 2.3**).

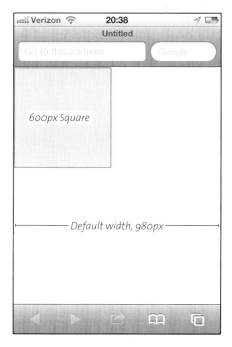

FIGURE 2.3 A 600px square as it would appear in the default viewport.

So, for example, if I say

```
<meta name="viewport" content="width=600">
```

an element that's defined as 600px wide in CSS would fill the screen horizontally on initial page load, or when the user double-taps to zoom out (**Figure 2.4**).

FIGURE 2.4 A 600px
square as it would
appear with a viewport
width of 600px.

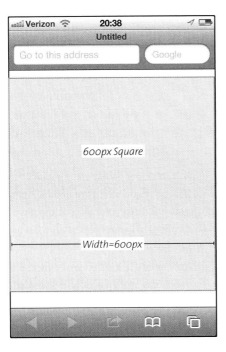

PX VS. EM

Although there are several units defined in the CSS 2 and CSS 3 specifications, most developers restrict themselves to two: em and px. One em always represents the value of the current font-size. If the font-size is 12px, 1em is equal to 12px. One px is (historically) one pixel on the screen. Around 2005 the use of the em became very popular, because of the wide use of the browser ability to change the font size. Because an em is defined relative to the font size, a layout could easily be made to adapt to the user-selected font size.

Since IE7 however, browsers have made full-page zooming rather than font resizing their default behavior. The px is now the most popular choice among designers thanks to its simplicity. Pixels are easier to communicate and easier to understand. Units like the em or underused ex have their uses, mostly for typesetting rather than layout, but the px is the simplest unit for laying out a pixel-perfect web page.

The viewport is a virtual window. The edges of the viewport, rather than the browser, become the edges of the window.

In addition to a pixel value, the viewport width and height accept two keywords: `device-width` and `device-height`, which ostensibly return the actual dimensions of the device screen in pixels (**Figure 2.5**).

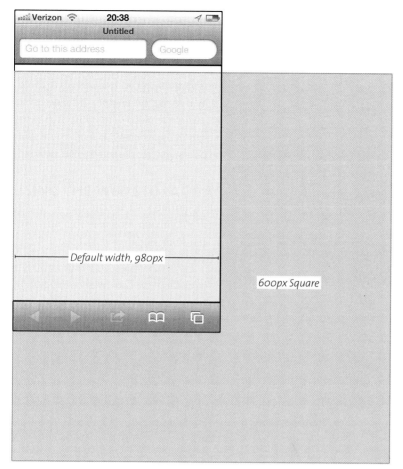

FIGURE 2.5 A 600px square as it would appear with a viewport width of device-width, or 320px.

Default width, 980px

600px Square

TABLE 2.1 Viewport properties (supported in Android 2.2+, iOS 1.0+, Mobile Firefox 1.1+)

PROPERTY	DESCRIPTION
width	Sets the width of the viewport in pixels. The default is 980. The allowed range is 200 to 10,000.
height	Sets the height of the viewport in pixels. The default is calculated from the width and the device aspect ratio. The allowed range is 223 to 10,000.
initial-scale	Sets the initial scale of the viewport. The default is calculated to fit the page in the viewable area. The range is set by the minimum-scale and maximum-scale properties.
maximum-scale	Sets the maximum scale of the viewport. The default is 5.0. The allowed range is 0 to 10.0.
user-scaleable	Determines whether the user can scale the viewport. Also prevents scrolling when text is being entered.

On the Birds of California site, the width of the viewport will be the same as the width of the device, which is convenient from a design standpoint and will be very helpful when we start making sure the CSS adapts to different devices. On an iPhone 1 through 4s the value of device-width (assuming vertical orientation) is 320px.

HIGH-DENSITY DISPLAYS

With each generation of mobile devices since the iPhone and the viewport tag arrived, device resolutions have increased. Resolutions are now so high that the actual pixels are too small for a human to distinguish—even with a microscope. Had the spec not changed, web pages with their viewport set to device-width would have ended up with very tiny interfaces on mobile displays. On the iPhone 4, the first device with this type of display, the elements would have been half the size they were on older iPhones.

Once again Apple was the first manufacturer to bring a high-density display to market. To keep web developers sane, Apple decided to continue to report a value of 320 for device-width on the iPhone 4, even though the screen was 640 physical pixels across. Android devices followed suit. Their devices were more complex because they give their users more control over how things are displayed. (Android Chrome has the not very useful target-densitydpi viewport property to support this. See the Android developer documentation for more information.) The devices have all settled on returning a value for device-width that is what the developers of the device consider the ideal dimensions for laying out interface elements. The values vary quite a bit, so when we create a web layout with a viewport width of device-width, we need to make sure the layout can handle some stretching, much like a liquid layout on a traditional desktop site.

What does all this mean for Birds of California? Because the designer provided us with a mobile layout that neatly filled the viewport, we can use device-width:

```
<meta name="viewport" content="width=device-width">
```

In most cases this is the best value, because it allows an interface that will fit the user's device perfectly, and we won't have to worry about it breaking at certain widths.

RESPONSIVE CSS

On this book's companion website, touch-interfaces.com, you can download two CSS files:

- Eric Meyer's reset.css file. There are a few "reset" CSS styles out there. I strongly recommend using them; it's better to start with a clean slate than to try and fight with the browser style defaults.

- A style sheet (birds.css) for the Birds of California site. Birds.css starts with the desktop styles. You'll probably recognize a fairly simple, two-column liquid layout. On the desktop the content area is liquid and the sidebar, containing the navigation buttons, is fixed.

  Listing 2.3 shows the base styles.

LISTING 2.3 Base styles

```css
html {
    background: #fff;
    color: #000;
}

a {
    color: green;
    text-decoration: none;
}

p {
    margin-bottom: 10px;
}

h2 {
    font-size: 20px;
    margin: 4px;
}

i {
    font-style: italic;
}

.container {
    padding: 0 50px;
}

.bd {
    font-family: Helvetica, "Helvetica Neue", Arial, sans-serif ;
}

.hero-img {
    max-width: 100%;
}

.nav-li {
    display: inline-block;
    background: #5e49ff;
```

```css
    border: 3px solid #8a7bfd;
    width: 120px;
    margin-bottom: 10px;
}

.nav-li .nav-link {
    color: #fff;
    padding: 4px;
}

.header {
    width: 100%;
    height: 60px;
    background: #000;
    padding: 0;
    font-size: 38px;
    font-weight: bold;

}

.header .title{
    color: #fff;
    padding: 10px;
    text-align: left;
}

/* Allow the image to grow proportionally inside its container */
.hero-shot {
    width: 50%;
    float: left;
    margin-right: 10px;
}

.sidebar {
    position: absolute;
    padding: 10px;
    top: 60px;
    width: 150px;
}
```

```
.main {

  margin: 10px 10px 10px 150px;

}

.footer {
  width: 100%;
}
```

You might notice that the seagulls image has a max-width of 100%, and the enclosing container (.hero-shot) has a relative width. This is the simplest way to create so-called responsive images, that is, images that will automatically scale proportionally to the container width. In this case the width will always be half the width of the text block.

This responsive image technique has a major downside: the user's device will certainly have to download too many bytes. We'll revisit this image in the next chapter.

CREATING BREAKPOINTS

As mentioned earlier, we'll be using the same markup for both the mobile and desktop versions of the Birds of California site. The design was made with this in mind; the layout and design will adapt to fit the size of the user's device. We can do this by creating breakpoints: pixel widths that trigger the design to change to fit different screen widths. For Birds of California we'll create two breakpoints: 800px for tablets and 480px for mobile phones.

This means if the screen is at least 801px wide, we'll apply the default styles listed in the stylesheet. We'll create specific styles for tablets with screen widths of 481px up to and including 800px. And we'll create additional styles for mobile phones with screen widths of 480px wide or less.

If you've never done it before, the idea of changing the design to fit the screen width sounds daunting. Thankfully, media queries make it possible to create a design that adapts without using JavaScript at all.

MEDIA QUERIES

Since CSS 2 became ubiquitous, developers have been able to serve different style sheets to different media via the media attribute of the link tag. This has most commonly been used to specify a separate "print" style sheet. For example:

```
<!-- this stylesheet is for the screen -->
<link rel="stylesheet" media="screen" href="styles.css">

<!-- This stylesheet is for printing -->
<link rel="stylesheet" media="print" href="print-styles.css">
```

CSS3 provides a much more powerful syntax that lets you filter style sheets on many more criteria. Rather than just a media type, you can specify a *media query*. A media query consists of a media type and one or more expressions. When evaluated, a media query resolves to either true or false. If true, the style sheet is applied.

A media query can start with a Boolean operator. Starting with "not" would negate the query—like using the ! operator in JavaScript. Most commonly, you will start with the only operator. The only operator can't be parsed by older browsers, effectively hiding the style sheet.

Next comes a media type. There are ten media types in the CSS 2.1 spec, but only `print` and `screen` are widely supported. Following the media type you specify an expression. For the Birds of California site, we'll change styles based on the screen width. This is accomplished with the `width` media feature. The `width` feature takes a value (specified in any valid CSS unit) for filtering purposes.

For example, this rule limits a style sheet to only narrow screens:

```
<link rel="stylesheet" media="only screen and (max-width: 480px)"
→ href="phone-styles.css">
```

And this rule limits a style sheet to only huge screens:

```
<link rel="stylesheet" media="only screen and (min-width: 2000px)"
→ href="phone-styles.css">
```

For the Birds of California site we'll use media queries to target the specific screen widths we've identified as breakpoints. So there are three style sheets:

```
<link rel="stylesheet" media="screen" href="birds.css">
<link rel="stylesheet" media="only screen and (max-width: 800px)"
→ href="tablet.css">
<link rel="stylesheet" media="only screen and (max-width: 480px)"
→ href="phone.css">
```

The pixel values here are based on what the browser chooses to report. Retina iPhones in vertical orientation, for example, are 320px wide for the purposes of media queries, regardless of the actual physical pixels on the screen.

NOTE: This chapter barely scratches the surface of media queries. Check out the Mozilla Development Network for a detailed explanation of the syntax (https://developer.mozilla.org/en-US/docs/CSS/Media_queries). For some examples, visit mediaqueri.es.

The really great thing about media queries is that we can use them outside the media property. We can also use them within the style sheet itself using the @media directive.

```
@media only screen and (max-width: 800px) {
    /* css that applies only in this case */
}
```

The syntax is the same as in the media parameter. The @media directive creates a block between the curly brackets. CSS within the brackets will only apply when the rule returns true, otherwise the browser will treat the CSS inside the block as if it didn't exist.

CREATING STYLES FOR BREAKPOINTS

For Birds of California we'll make additional styles for 800px-wide browsers and 480px-wide browsers. The designer has created another mock-up for the tablet view, moving the navigation to the top and centering the header to leave more room for copy. Otherwise the styles are the same (**Figure 2.6**).

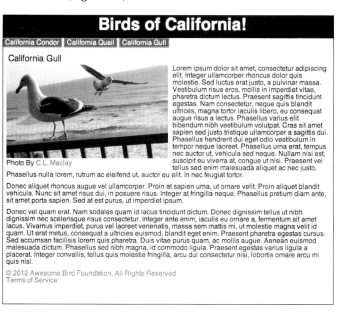

FIGURE 2.6 A tablet view of Birds of California.

Because the sidebar was first in the DOM we can simply assign it relative positioning and a width of auto to pop it back into the document flow. Then we can give the container a little less padding, as shown in **Listing 2.4**.

LISTING 2.4 Tablet styles

```
.container {
    padding: 0 10px;
}


.nav-li {
    width: auto; /* so all the text fits */
}
```

```
.sidebar {
  position:relative; /* back in the flow */
  top: 0;
  width: auto;
  padding: 0;
  text-align: center;
}

.header .title {
  text-align: center;
}

.main {
  margin: 0;
}
```

A desktop user who resizes her browser will also see the styles that apply to them, based on the width of her browser. If you'd rather these styles apply only to physical device widths, use `max-device-width` or `min-device-width`.

As you can see, styles cascade normally with media queries. The phone mock-up shown in Figure 2.2 calls for a slightly different layout. **Listing 2.5** shows the phone styles.

LISTING 2.5 Phone styles

```
.container {
  padding: 0;
}

.main {
  margin: 0;
}

.contcnt {
  margin: 10px 10px;
}

.nav-li {
  font-size: 12px;
}
```

```
.hero-shot {
    float: none;
    width: 100%;
    height: 100px;
    overflow: hidden;
    position: relative;
}

.header .title {
    font-size: 24px;
    text-align: left;
}

.hero-shot .caption {
    position: absolute;
    bottom: 5px;
    margin: 0;

}

.hero-shot .caption, .hero-shot .caption a {
    color: #000;
    color: rgba(255,255,255,0.5);
}

}
```

The complete markup is available on the website as Listing 2.5. If you try this page in a desktop browser, you'll see the styles change as you resize the browser window.

WRAPPING UP

In this chapter you learned how to use media queries to create design breakpoints. You also learned about the `viewport` meta element and virtual pixels. Remember that mobile browsers are not resizable and there is no standard width. Any layout that will work on mobile must be flexible.

CHAPTER 3

Speeding Up
the First Load

The first contact users have with a site is when they begin to form an opinion about whether or not it's "slow." If the first load feels sluggish, particularly on a mobile connection, users may go away before it finishes and never come back. Making that first load fast is the most fundamental thing a developer needs to do when making a site responsive.

The speed of the first load is measured in "time to first byte," that is, the time from when the user requests the page to when the first byte starts to come down from the server. Although this is important to know, measure, and optimize, in the vast majority of cases this is not the cause of first load slowness. The problem commonly lies on the front end. PageSpeed, YSlow, and a myriad of tools and services exist to solve these issues.

HOW THE BROWSER LOADS A PAGE

Before going into detail about how to optimize, let's review how a browser loads a page.

RESOLVING THE DOMAIN

First the browser needs to know the IP address of the website. It makes a request to a DNS server with the domain name, which returns the IP address. To reduce load on DNS servers, and to improve performance, DNS lookups are cached by the browser and the device. They're also usually cached by routers and proxies between the device and the server. This is the reason that changes to DNS records can take several days to take effect.

MAKING THE REQUEST

Next, the browser opens a TCP connection to the server whose IP it got from the DNS lookup and then sends the request. The request contains the URL, information about the browser, the type of data it will accept (encoding and language), and all the cookies relevant for the page, including both domain and path cookies.

DOWNLOADING THE RESPONSE

The browser begins downloading the response. As the response streams, the browser identifies additional resources in the HTML as it is parsed. The browser begins to fetch these resources.

RENDERING THE PAGE

The browser starts rendering the page as soon as it can. If there are CSS or script files found, the browser waits until those files are loaded and parsed (and executed, in the case of Java-Script) to render the content after those files are linked.

WHY ARE PAGES SLOW?

Why are pages slow to load? Consider the following culprits:

- Number of HTTP requests
- Byte count
- Blocking rendering while waiting
- Latency
- Poor cacheability

THE WEBKIT TIMELINE

Aside from a good text editor, the most important tools for mobile web developers are the WebKit Developer Tools. You can get a lot of work done just using Chrome or Safari on your desktop before you get serious about testing and optimizing on an actual device. Using the device can be unwieldy, so particularly in the building stage of development, WebKit is a great tool. If you have a Mac and iOS 6, the Safari Web Inspector becomes amazingly powerful (more on this later). When diagnosing performance issues, start in the network pane. In Safari, this is hiding in the Instrument view called Network Requests (**Figure 3.1**).

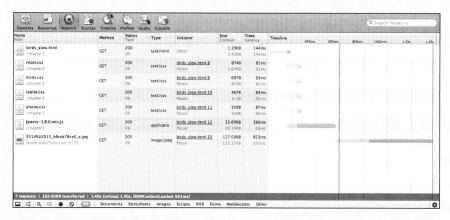

FIGURE 3.1 The WebKit Developer Tools.

There's a lot of great information here, but for now we'll focus on the Network tab, which features a beautiful waterfall graph that shows us everything we need to know about the loading of the page. **Figure 3.2** shows how the Birds of California site loaded.

FIGURE 3.2 The waterfall graph for Birds of California.

The light color in the bars represents latency and the dark represents download. You can see that none of the external resources were loaded until the browser parsed that part of the page. You can also see how it didn't start fetching the image until after it had downloaded jQuery. It took 1.4 seconds on my fast connection at home to get the page loaded. The top bar shows latency (back-end performance) wasn't bad. But this page was pretty slow for such a simple page.

NUMBER OF HTTP REQUESTS

Every external resource on your page requires a separate HTTP request. An HTTP request isn't as simple as just downloading the data; there's a certain amount of overhead in every request. So if all requests were made one after another, many small files would be much, much slower than one large file.

Browsers, of course, can download multiple files in parallel. If you look back at Figure 3.2 you'll see that most of the assets were downloaded in parallel. The HTTP/1.1 spec recommends two parallel downloads and modern browsers can download many more. Safari on iOS supports up to six requests in parallel *per hostname*. By adding additional hostnames (perhaps by setting up aliases or subdomains) you can download even more files in parallel. Nevertheless, each request must still pay the penalty of the HTTP overhead.

It may seem bizarre that parallelism doesn't help here. Parallelism doesn't ultimately overcome the cost of overhead because executing two downloads simultaneously isn't twice as fast as just one. Not only does creating a new request have cost, but each download has cost in terms of CPU and memory.

For larger files, such as large images, the equation changes. Because the bulk of the request time on these files is generally the download, more parallelism is better. For that reason (and some others) it makes sense to serve images and assets from separate domains from your site. At Yahoo!, Steve Souders and the YSlow team found that creating two aliases for a domain to allow more parallel downloads resulted in a distinct performance improvement for large files.

As you can imagine, because there is still a parallel request limit, at some point the browser must wait for requests to finish before starting the next downloads. That means that if your site is all served from the same domain it is necessarily slower at first load than one spread across domains. However, because each extra domain requires an extra DNS lookup, adding domains eventually makes things slower. Using at least two but less than five domains is the rule of thumb from YSlow.

SPDY AND HTTP PIPELINING

You may have asked yourself why you have to pay the HTTP overhead penalty for each request. If all the requests are to the same domain, why not just leave the connection open and stream down more data?

If you did, you're not the only one. Two competing solutions are emerging. SPDY (pronounced "speedy") is a new protocol developed by Google that is intended to replace HTTP. The other is pipelining, specified in HTTP/1.1, but not implemented in all browsers yet. Both would allow the browser to use the same connection for multiple assets, overcoming the limitations of parallelism and making multiple smaller files almost certainly superior to the current best practice of fewer, larger files.

Another consideration is browser cookies. If a cookie matches the domain or path of the request, it is sent (that is, uploaded) with every request. So if you set several kilobytes of cookies on your domain with the first request, every other request to that domain will include those bytes be sent, uncompressed, with the header of that request. The server also has to read those cookies before it can read the body of the request. Cookies can turn a tiny request into a very large one.

BYTE COUNT

The next thing that slows pages down is probably the most obvious: the size of the download. Pages always start small, but when you add JavaScript libraries, styles, and most of all images, pages can get orders of magnitude larger. Anything you can do to reduce the overall size of the files downloaded is time well spent.

BLOCKING RENDERING WHILE WAITING

In this book we'll talk a lot about perceived performance. Some things don't actually speed things up, but they make things seem much faster to the user. User feedback is critical to responsiveness. When the user is staring at a blank page while the browser loads, he can't tell if the connection has been lost or if the page is slow. If the user can see your page, even if all the assets aren't loaded, the perceived performance will be much better. For example: script tags block rendering of the HTML that follows it until the script has been fetched, parsed, and executed. When you put four or five external lines of JavaScript in the head, the user is forced to wait until all of those scripts are loaded before he sees anything at all.

LATENCY

Network connections are measured by bandwidth (bits) and latency (milliseconds). Latency is the delay added to a request by the connection. A typical home network connection might have a download speed of 8 megabits per second and a latency of around 15ms. A typical 3G connection might have a 500 kbps download speed and 100ms of latency. So not only is the download speed much slower, but the latency also is much higher.

Latency is annoying for users because although once a download starts it might be reasonably fast, the wait for the download to start can be quite painful. High latency dramatically increases the problems caused by large numbers of requests by adding a lot of time to each round trip. A header redirect, for example, might not be noticeable on a good broadband connection. But on a mobile device over 3G it might add 200ms to the page load. 200ms is a very noticeable delay.

POOR CACHEABILITY

We'll talk more about optimizing caching in the next chapter. For now, just remember that several of the PageSpeed and YSlow rules are designed to make sure that your cache is set up right so the browser doesn't end up re-fetching data it already has.

SPEEDING UP WITH YSLOW AND PAGESPEED

So far we've scratched the surface of how page loads end up slow. Now let's look at how to make page loads *fast*. Luckily there are two excellent tools (both associated with web performance expert Steve Souders) to help analyze your website for performance problems.

YSLOW

YSlow is a tool developed by the Yahoo! Exceptional Performance team way back in 2007. It compares your website against a set of best practices. The YSlow website lists 34 rules and the tool tests for 23 of them. The full list with excellent documentation is available from the YSlow website at developer.yahoo.com/yslow/.

Figure 3.3 shows what happens when we run YSlow against the Birds of California site. I've added a link to jQuery in the head just to make the example a little more realistic.

FIGURE 3.3 The YSlow report for the Birds of California site.

The site gets a "B," mostly because it's so simple. There are only four external CSS files and one JavaScript file, so YSlow gave that section an "A" but still made some recommendations. It got an "F" for two categories: "Add expires headers" and "Use a content delivery network." We'll talk more about expires headers in the next chapter. One of the sticking points about YSlow since it was first introduced has been its recommendation regarding a content delivery network. That's one of the main reasons YSlow offers a special "Small Site or Blog" rule set.

A *content delivery network (CDN)* is a service that lets you serve certain (usually static) content from "edge servers": servers located in many, many places, hopefully not very far from the end user. This is usually used for images, JavaScript, and CSS files because they're unlikely to change.

These servers usually cache resources. If your JavaScript, CSS, and image files are on a CDN like Akamai or Amazon CloudFront, the files might be cached in a data center only a few miles from the end user. That short distance is critical, because one of the major causes of latency is the speed of light.

The speed of light in glass (like fiber optic cables) is a little slower than in a vacuum, so a round trip in 1,000 kilometers of fiber is about 11 milliseconds. The server hosting my website (which I'm using for testing the Birds of California site) is in Dallas. Assuming I was connected to a straight fiber optic cable to that server I would expect 22 milliseconds of additional latency, just because of the distance. In practice the network between me and that server is quite a bit slower, so testing the latency to that server via ping shows that there's about 50 milliseconds of network latency. A CDN puts the server much closer to the user. When I ping an Akamai or CloudFront server I get something like 17ms of latency. Obviously there is a huge benefit.

You don't upload files to a CDN. A CDN works by fetching content from your server and then caching it close to the user fetching it. So the first user to request the file gets a small benefit because the file is transmitted over dedicated lines, but he still has to pay the price in latency caused by distance. Additional users in the same basic location will then benefit from the cached version. If your site gets decent traffic, you will benefit.

The overall effectiveness of an edge cache (and all caching systems) is based on the "hit rate" for your cache. If most requests to the CDN cache result in an empty cache (a miss) the benefit is limited. This could happen because you have lots of different URLs that every user doesn't see, or because your traffic is low enough and geographically spread enough that the edge cache is rarely primed. For low traffic sites a CDN won't help that much. However, putting your static files on a separate domain without cookies will always help. So if you can, do it.

PAGESPEED

When Steve Souders left Yahoo! he joined Google and became part of the team working on PageSpeed. PageSpeed builds on YSlow, adding more rules and more features. Most importantly, PageSpeed has a set of rules for mobile.

I ran the Birds of California site through the online tool using the mobile mode (**Figure 3.4**).

As you can see, the PageSpeed score is much worse than YSlow. That's great, because I suspected that the "A" from YSlow didn't reflect a lot of optimizations that could be done. In general YSlow is a good start, and PageSpeed is where to go when you want to move to the next level of optimization.

FIGURE 3.4 The Page-Speed mobile insights report for *Birds of California*.

Overview

The page Birds of California got an overall PageSpeed Score of **46** (out of 100). Learn more

This PageSpeed Report is generated for this page as it appears on mobile devices. To get a PageSpeed Report for desktop clients, view the desktop report instead.

Suggestion Summary

Click on the rule names to see suggestions for improvement.

- **High priority.** These suggestions represent the largest potential performance wins for the least development effort. However, there are no high priority suggestions for this site. Good job!

- **Medium priority.** These suggestions may represent smaller wins or much more work to implement. You should address these items next:
  Serve scaled images, Inline Small CSS, Defer parsing of JavaScript, Leverage browser caching

- **Low priority.** These suggestions represent the smallest wins. You should only be concerned with these items after you've handled the higher-priority ones:
  Optimize images, Specify a character set

- **Experimental rules.** These suggestions are experimental, but do not affect the overall PageSpeed score. Consider these items as points to an area to explore, but your mileage might vary:
  Use an Application Cache, Avoid a character set in the meta tag, Eliminate unnecessary reflows

- **Already done!.** There are no suggestions for these rules, since this page already follows these best practices. Good job!

PageSpeed groups rules into six basic categories. Extensive documentation for each is available on the PageSpeed site (https://developers.google.com/speed/docs/best-practices/rules_intro):

- Optimizing caching—keeping your application's data and logic off the network altogether
- Minimizing round-trip times—reducing the number of serial request-response cycles
- Minimizing request overhead—reducing upload size
- Minimizing payload size—reducing the size of responses, downloads, and cached pages
- Optimizing browser rendering—improving the browser's layout of a page
- Optimizing for mobile—tuning a site for the characteristics of mobile networks and mobile devices

Currently the mobile categories contain just two recommendations: "Defer parsing of JavaScript" and "Make landing page redirects cacheable." We'll talk about the first shortly, but the second recommendation deserves special mention, because it's such a widespread issue. A common practice is to redirect mobile users to a separate mobile website (Flickr, for example, redirects mobile users from www.flickr.com to m.flickr.com). This is a very expensive practice, because redirects add an additional round trip. (A redirect sends a message in the header to the browser telling it to fetch a different resource at a different location.)

This effect can be mitigated somewhat by allowing the client to cache the redirect. You can do this by including an "expires" header (this header was set on August 26, 2012):

```
HTTP/1.1 302 Moved Temporarily
Date: Mon, 27 Aug 2012 22:34:05 GMT
Expires: Sat, 25 Aug 2012 22:34:05 GMT
Cache-Control: private, max-age=86400
```

I've included a Cache-Control: private, set expires in the past, and left the max-age to one day in the future. Why not just set it to the far future? And why cache-control: private? I'm concerned about proxies. Many users access the Internet via proxies that cache things closer to the user to improve performance. When making a redirect cacheable we want to make sure that mobile users accessing the Internet via the same proxy cause desktop users to be redirected to the mobile site.

PageSpeed also has more interesting tools and a service that rewrites your page for you. Check out the PageSpeed website (developers.google.com/speed/pagespeed/)—it's an amazing resource.

SOLVING COMMON PROBLEMS

Birds of California isn't a terrible site in terms of front-end performance, but it could be much better than it is. The first step is measurement. We've already discussed the WebKit Developer Tools. Another valuable tool is Charles proxy (Charlesproxy.com). Charles is a local tool that lets you inspect every request, add breakpoints to requests, and simulate low-bandwidth situations. When the developer tools don't give you enough information about HTTP, Charles comes to the rescue.

To begin, open Charles proxy. To get a real sense of what this connection is like we'll use Charles to simulate a typical 3G connection.

Click the Proxy menu and then choose Throttle Settings (**Figure 3.5**).

The 3G preset is fine for our purposes (**Figure 3.6**).

Now we can refresh the page to see the damage (**Figure 3.7**).

FIGURE 3.5 Configuring Throttle Settings.

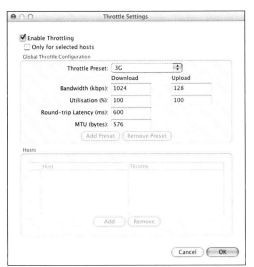

FIGURE 3.6 (Left) The Throttle Settings dialog with the 3G preset selected.

FIGURE 3.7 (Below) The throttled waterfall graph for Birds of California.

The page takes three and a half seconds to load. Obviously the high latency is problematic, but there's a lot of room for improvement. You can clearly see in the timeline where the problems are:

- There are too many requests.
- The image doesn't even start loading until jQuery is finished loading.
- The image is huge!

Our clever technique from the previous chapter has given us an adaptive image, but we're downloading way more bytes than we need.

Now let's go through the issues on the site one by one.

TOO MANY REQUESTS

For mobile, even with media queries, it's pretty trivial to combine all the CSS files into one file and one request. Instead of using a "media" parameter in the link element we can use the CSS media query syntax:

```
<link rel="stylesheet" media="only screen and (max-width: 800px)"
 href="tablet.css">
```

Becomes

```
@media only screen and (max-width: 800px) {
}
```

inside the CSS file. By combining the CSS files we end up with a combo.css that includes all the CSS we need:

```
[Reset.css content]
[Birds.css]
@media only screen and (max-width: 800px) {
[Tablet.css content]
}
@media only screen and (max-width: 480px) {
[Phone.css content]
}
```

Let's see how that improves this situation (**Figure 3.8**).

Well, darn, that didn't really help at all. The difference, if any, was quite small, certainly not the full second or so we'd like to shave off the load. Something to consider now is that we're looking at the empty cache experience—with good reason. Mobile browser caches are very limited (more on this in the next chapter)—you can't count much on them.

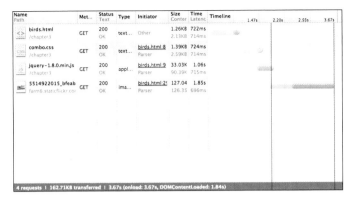

FIGURE 3.8 The effect of combining all of the CSS.

Only collecting real data will tell you for sure how often a user comes to your site with a primed cache. (Data collected by the YSlow team in 2007 found that about 20 percent of all page views are empty cache; on mobile it is certainly much higher.) We'll discuss caching strategies more in the next chapter, but for now let's go ahead and inline the styles. We'll also remove any white space, to save a few precious bytes.

THE CRITICAL PATH

Unfortunately, inlining styles still won't improve the situation much. When looking at the waterfall graph we're trying to figure out what the "critical path" is. For this site, aside from the image, it's apparent that jQuery is a big problem. In fact, the image doesn't even start loading until jQuery is finished. If you recall, that's because script tags block rendering until they are loaded and parsed. Because the image tag isn't in the document until after the script tag, the browser can't start fetching it until after jQuery has fully loaded.

The quickest solution to this problem is to put the script on the bottom of the page rather than the top. That way while the script is being fetched the user won't be looking at a blank page, and any resources inlined will be fetched in parallel with the script. Doing this with the Birds of California site dramatically improves things (**Figure 3.9**).

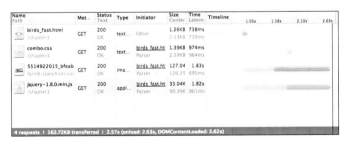

FIGURE 3.9 The effect of moving JavaScript to the bottom.

As you can see the image now starts before the script, and the two load in parallel. Based on further testing of this version of the page, with inline CSS and JavaScript on the bottom, loading is about a second faster on average. More importantly the user sees content in under two seconds. Users don't measure performance by how long it takes for all the resources to load. They perceive performance based on how long it takes for them to see the content they want.

THE IMAGE IS HUGE!

Looking again, you can see things still aren't rosy. That image is sticking out like a sore thumb. The uncompressed text of this book is about 250 kilobytes. The image of the gull we've been using so far is about half that size. When trying to reduce byte count for a mobile site, images are usually the biggest problem. Even worse, the recent generations of phones have very high-density screens. An iPhone 4 has landscape pixel dimensions of 960 x 640 and the Samsung Galaxy S III has a whopping 1280 x 720. Mobile users are generally on slower connections, but their high-density screens demand equal or higher-resolution images than their desktop counterparts.

Luckily the Birds of California site design doesn't ask for any images for the user interface. If it had, we'd need to replace every image we could with CSS gradients, box shadows, and round corners where possible. Still, the design has that huge image. From a user standpoint, he would like to download only the size image he needs. At Flickr, image sizes are all created automatically from the large images that users upload. Because of this exact problem, Flickr generates 11 different sizes for each image, including double resolution versions of common sizes for high-density displays.

Most websites aren't Flickr. For this website, we don't have a multimillion dollar system for quickly generating different images. Instead I just have Photoshop and if this website is going to be comprehensive, it will probably have pictures of quite a few birds. Using one high-resolution image scaled in the browser saves a lot of labor, but the user pays the price. If you can't reasonably generate every size you need, you can make some compromises. For this site, I'll optimize for what I *think* is the most common case.

NOTE Nothing is better than real data for making decisions. You can create simple reporting tools to gather numbers on what people are doing, such as landscape versus portrait, screen resolution, and so on. Most analytics tools give you ways to either get this data in normal reports, or they allow you to record custom data. Keep in mind that most mobile users are on metered connections, which means they have to pay for the bytes they use. Large images for Retina screens might seem great, but be judicious. If you're asking your users to pay for big images they should really be necessary. Among other reasons, this is why the Birds of California mobile design has a cropped image.

Most phone users will probably view the Birds of California site in portrait mode. Since the design doesn't offer any extra features in landscape mode, I'm OK with giving those users a less than ideal, but acceptable view.

For the tablet, the images we already made are fine. For the phone, we'll generate just two images for the cropped view: normal and Retina. Previously I defined the cropped image to be 100px and fill the width of the screen. A portrait Galaxy S III is 720px across, the most of any common device. That means the cropped seagull image needs to be 720px across. It also needs to be tall enough to accommodate a variety of aspect ratios. I defined it as 100

CSS pixels high, which means at least 200 physical pixels to support Retina screens. On the iPhone, the image is scaled down to only 640px across, making the image on the Samsung 12.5% wider. To prevent the image from being too short, we'll make the image 12.5% bigger, which is 225 pixels. So in the end, we'll have two images, one 720 x 225, one 360 x 113 for lower-density screens. In landscape mode this won't be big enough for a perfect Retina image, but it's still better than a 480px image would be, and for our purposes should be enough. We could create two more images to handle landscape, but in this case I think that's unnecessary and I'm willing to accept the trade-off. See **Figure 3.10**.

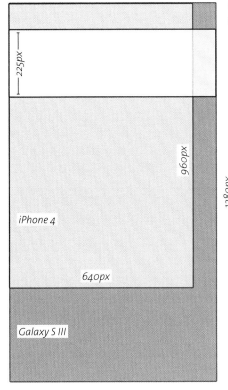

FIGURE 3.10 The extreme dimensions the image must support.

225px

960px

1280px

iPhone 4

640px

Galaxy S III

720px

The next trick is to make sure the large image is not downloaded by mobile clients; only the correct image for that device should be downloaded. There are several techniques, but I strongly prefer using only CSS to achieve it. Again, media queries come to the rescue, giving us a way to override styles based on the properties of the display. To make this technique work we'll convert the `<img>` tag we used before into a `<div>` with a background image. We could also use an image tag with a tiny transparent GIF for the `src`, if we prefered to be more semantic in the code. Of course, if the `src` doesn't describe the actual image being displayed, then we've let semantics go anyway.

The new "hero image" markup looks like this:

```html
<div class="hero-shot">
    <a href="http://www.flickr.com/photos/catlantis/5514922015/">
      <div role="img"
        aria-label="California gull flying"
        class="hero-img">
      </div>
      <p class="caption">Photo By
    <a href="http://www.flickr.com/photos/catlantis/5514922015/">
      C.L. Maclay
    </a>
      </p>
</div>
```

Using a `<div>` here broke semantics. But we've brought it back with a technology called Web Accessibility Initiative-Accessible Rich Internet Applications (WAI-ARIA). ARIA augments HTML with additional attributes designed to explicitly assign semantic and other information to elements.

Converting the "alt" attribute of the image to an ARIA label lets us restore semantics, at least for screen readers and other assistive technologies. Previously we set a `max-width` of 100%, forcing the image to grow proportionally with the enclosing element:

```css
.hero-shot {
    width: 50%;
    float: left;
    margin-right: 10px;
}
.hero-img {
    max-width: 100%;
}
```

Unfortunately this trick doesn't work with a `div` tag. It works with an image because an image has a natural size in DOM. If you don't specify a width and height for an image, it will take on the native dimensions of the source image. If we change the markup without changing the styles, the .hero-shot element collapses to zero height. The first thing we'll do is set up the background image. We don't want the image to grow beyond the native size, so we'll specify a `max-width` as well. We'll also set up the width to be 100% again, so that it grows as before:

```css
.hero-img {
    max-width: 640px;
    width: 100%;
    background: url(gull-640x360.jpg);
}
```

This still will have no height, however. Somehow we need to set a height that is a percentage of the width. In this case the photo is 640 x 360, so we need the height to be 56% of the width. You can't normally do math in CSS, but in this case we're lucky. The CSS padding of an element, when specified in percent, actually refers to the percentage of the width of the element, even for vertical padding!

So we can do this:

```
.hero-img {
    max-width: 640px;
    width: 100%;
    height: 0;
    padding-bottom: 56%;
    background-size: 100%;
    background: url(gull-640x360.jpg);
}
```

Now the `<div>` will scale as before, this time with a CSS background image rather than an `img src`. This is a nice trick, but it doesn't actually solve the problem at hand, which is downloading too many bytes. So how do we solve that problem?

First, let's tackle the issue of different image sizes for different layouts. As before we can use media queries, but this time we'll vary the image by media query. For desktop browsers, using the large size is fine, because bandwidth and memory aren't as much of an issue, and users on desktop resize their browser windows.

```
@media only screen and (min-width: 800px) {
    .hero-img {
        background: url(gull-640x360.jpg);
    }
}
```

On a tablet, the image is a maximum size of 390 x 219, a lot smaller than the image we created before. Unlike on a desktop, users really have only two browser orientation choices: landscape and portrait.

The biggest tablet browser width (in CSS px) that we need to support is 1024. This size is big enough that the desktop view will look great, and the image is big enough to look good in the 50% size, even on an iPad with a Retina display.

Now onto the phone. The cropped image keeps the same inner div, but the containing element is set to 100px tall as before. All we need to do is change the image src:

```
@media only screen and (max-width: 480px) {
    .hero-img {
        background: url(gull-360x112.jpg);
    }
}
```

We'd be done now, if it weren't for the fact that many newer phones have high-density displays. There are two approaches to load a separate image for Retina or HiDPI devices. The simplest is the new image-set CSS function, currently available only in iOS 6, Chromium 20, Safari 6, and the latest versions of Android Chrome. It's also a proposal, not a standard, so it will probably change before it can be used without a prefix. With image-set you can define different URLs based on the device pixel density. An iPhone 4 or 5 is 2x because there are two physical pixels for every CSS pixel. A Galaxy S II is 1.5.

The syntax is simple:

```
@media only screen and (max-width: 480px) {
    .hero-img {
        background: url(gull-720x225.jpg); /*fallback for user
                                agents that don't support
                                image-set.*/
        background: -webkit-image-set(
            url(gull-360x112.jpg) 1x,
            url(gull-720x225.jpg) 1.5x,
            url(gull-720x225.jpg) 2x
        );
    }
}
```

This is WebKit-only, prefixed, and there's an uglier but equally effective approach. Media queries also allow specifying a device-pixel-ratio. You can target all high-density devices with a simple media query:

```
@media only screen and (min-device-pixel-ratio : 1.5) {
    .hero-img {
        background:  url(gull-720x225.jpg);
    }
}
```

Well, you'll be able to as soon as device-pixel-ratio is available unprefixed. For now you'll need to write the same block again for each vendor prefix (media queries do not support multiple rules with commas). The syntax for Firefox is *not* a typo. The actual syntax for Firefox is min--moz-device-pixel-ratio.

```
/* webkit */
@media only screen and (-webkit-min-device-pixel-ratio: 1.5){
    /* Css */
}
/* firefox mobile. */
```

```
@media only screen and (min--moz-device-pixel-ratio: 1.5) {
    /* Css */
}
/* opera */
@media only screen and (-o-min-device-pixel-ratio: 3/2) {
    /* Css */
}
```

Like I said, uglier but effective.

PULLING IT ALL TOGETHER

Let's pull all this together and see how good a job we can do. We put styles inline, JavaScript at the bottom, and optimized the images. When we load the site up in Chrome (with the window as narrow as possible so we download the smallest image), there's a dramatic improvement (**Figure 3.11**).

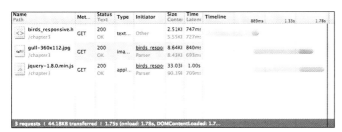

FIGURE 3.11 The Birds of California website, fully optimized.

We broke the two-second barrier, and it was relatively painless. It's good practice to keep an eye on the timeline, and run your site through PageSpeed every so often so that any major performance issues stand out right away.

WRAPPING UP

In this chapter you learned how to hit all the basics of speeding up the first page load, and dug into the complexities of serving images to a variety of devices. We'll come back to these simple concepts throughout the book, because even though everything else matters, the biggest part of making your site seem fast is that first page load. In the next chapter we'll look at how to speed load up the next time your users visit.

CHAPTER 4

Speeding Up
the Next Visit

So much about computing performance depends on caching. Fundamentally, caching is putting data somewhere after you get it the first time so you can access it much more quickly the next time. On the web, we want to take advantage of caching as often as possible to speed up users' subsequent visits to the site, keeping in mind that their next visit is quite frequently within seconds of their first, when they ask for another page.

On mobile, as much as anywhere, we want to make the best possible use of caching. The main tools we have for caching on touch devices are the normal browser cache, localStorage, and the application cache. In this chapter we'll look at normal browser cache, which isn't as good as it should be; LocalStorage, a newish API for persistent storage that's an incredibly powerful tool for manual caching; and the application cache.

CACHING IN HTTP

HTTP was designed with caching in mind. The cache we're most familiar with is the browser cache, but additional caching *proxies* often exist as well, and they follow the same rules defined in the specification. There are three ways to control HTTP caches:

- Freshness
- Validation
- Invalidation

FRESHNESS

Freshness, sometimes called the TTL (Time To Live), is the simplest. Using headers, caching agents are told how long to hold on to a cached resource before it should be considered stale and refetched. The simplest way this is handled is with the Expires header. You might remember that YSlow and PageSpeed recommend setting far-future Expires headers for static content.

The goal here is that so-called static assets (like CSS and JavaScript) are never fetched again, if possible. YSlow advises that you set an expiration some time in the distant future:

```
Expires: Thu, 15 Apr 2025 20:00:00 GMT
```

The intent is that the browser (or a caching proxy) will keep this file around until it runs out of room in cache.

VALIDATION

Validation provides a way for a caching agent to determine if a stale cache is actually still good, without requesting the full resource. The browser can make a request with an If-Modified-Since header. The server then can send a 304 Not Modified response and the browser uses the file already in the cache, rather than refetching from the server.

Another validation feature is the ETag. ETags are unique identifiers, usually hashes, which allow cache validation without dates by comparing a short string. The requesting agent makes a conditional request as well, but this time with an If-None-Match header containing the ETag. If the current content matches the client's ETag, then the server can again return a 304 response.

Validating the cache does require a full round-trip to the server. That is better than redownloading a file, but avoiding a round trip altogether is preferable. That's the reason for the far-future expiration date. If the cached item hasn't expired, then the browser won't attempt to validate it.

INVALIDATION

Browsers invalidate cached items after some actions, the most common being any non-GET request to the same URL.

WHAT IS NORMAL CACHE BEHAVIOR?

So what is the normal behavior of the browser cache, if you don't mess with the headers or do anything else? Most browsers have a maximum cache size. When that size is reached they begin removing items from the cache that were *least recently used*. So a cached item that hasn't been used in a long time will be purged, keeping items used more frequently.

The result of this algorithm is that what is purged is completely based on user behavior and there's no reliable way to predict how it will work. It's safe to assume that if you don't think about cache headers, then some browser will cache something you don't want cached and won't cache something you do.

OPTIMIZING FOR MOBILE

The browser cache is very important on a desktop computer, but not so much on touch devices.

In iOS 5, the browser cache is limited to 100 MB and *does not* persist between app launches. That means that if the phone restarts or the browser is killed or crashes, the entire cache is emptied when the browser starts again. Android 2.x's stock browser (still the most widely installed version by far) has a cache limit of just 5.7 MB, and that isn't per domain—that's total (**Table 4.1**).

TABLE 4.1 Persistent Cache Size by Browser

OS	BROWSER	MAX PERSISTENT SIZE
iOS 4.3	Mobile Safari	0
iOS 5.1.1	Mobile Safari	0
iOS 5.1.1	Chrome for iOS	200 MB +
Android 2.2	Android Browser	4 MB
Android 2.3	Android Browser	4 MB
Android 3.0	Android Browser	20 MB
Android 4.0–4.1	Chrome for Android	85 MB
Android 4.0–4.1	Android Browser	85 MB
Android 4.1	Firefox Beta	75 MB
BlackBerry OS 6	Browser	25 MB
BlackBerry OS 7	Browser	85 MB

* Adapted from research by Guy Podjarny (www.guypo.com)

It's very important to optimize the cacheability of your site. But the very limited size of the browser caches means that users will very often come to your site with an empty cache, so optimizing for that state should not be neglected.

A good header for a static resource looks something like this:

```
HTTP/1.1 200 OK
Content-Type: image/png
Last-Modified: Thu, 29 Mar 2012 23:53:57 GMT
Date: Tue, 11 Sep 2012 21:36:44 GMT
Expires: Wed, 11 Sep 2013 21:36:44 GMT
Cache-Control: public, max-age=31536000
```

`Cache-Control: public` makes sure that SSL resources can be cached by proxies. The max-age is one year (in seconds). The Expires date is also a year in the future.

In practice, it's a good idea to read up on how to configure your particular server so that the headers are correct. If you're working with separate back-end developers, gently remind them how important these values are.

For the actual content many major sites use `cache-control: private` to prevent any caching by proxies. For the Birds of California site, the content won't change that much, so on the server we can set up the cache headers to expire in one hour. We're using Nginx, so we can do that with the expires directive:

```
location / {
    expires 1h;
}
```

This results in a header that looks like this, assuming the site was accessed at 05:16:45 PST:

```
Last-Modified: Thu, 05 Jul 2012 17:15:35 PST
Connection: keep-alive
Vary: Accept-Encoding
Expires: Wed, 14 Nov 2012 06:16:46 PST
Cache-Control: max-age=3600
```

This prevents mobile users from refetching content too much during a browsing session, but ensures that the content is fresh, even for desktop users.

Another important thing to consider is web accelerators like Amazon Silk. Silk is the browser for the Kindle Fire tablets. Unlike a normal browser, Amazon Silk is a browser that lives both on the Kindle Fire and on Amazon servers. According to Amazon, much of the acceleration comes from pipelining and "predictive push," which means sending static resources to the browser before the browser even requests the resource. In this case Silk acts as a transparent HTTP proxy. A proxy may cache just like the browser, and it follows the same rules. So by sending the correct headers you're also improving performance for Kindle users.

USING WEB STORAGE

Browser makers, and Apple in particular, have left us with a less than ideal situation when it comes to the browser cache. But they and the W3C have given us something else that almost makes up for it: the web storage API. Web storage provides a persistent data store for the browser, in addition to cookies. Unlike cookies, 5 MB is available per domain in a simple key-value store. On iOS, WebStorage stores the text as a UTF-16 string, which means that each character takes twice as many bytes. So on iOS the total is actually 2.5 MB.

USING THE WEB STORAGE API

Web storage is accessed from two global variables: localStorage and sessionStorage. sessionStorage is a nonpersistent store; it's cleared between browsing sessions. It also isn't shared between tabs, so it's better suited to temporary storage of application data rather than caching. Other than that, localStorage and sessionStorage are the same.

Just like cookies, web storage access is limited by the same origin policy (a web page can only access web storage values set from the same domain) and if users reset their browsers all the data will be lost. One other small issue is that in iOS 5, web views in apps stored their web storage data in the same small space used for the browser cache, so they were hardly persistent. This has been fixed in iOS 6.

> **NOTE** LocalStorage should not be treated as secure. Like everything, the user can read and modify what is in localStorage.

The web storage API is very simple. The primary methods are localStorage.getItem('key'); localStorage.setItem('key', 'value'). key and value are stored as strings. If you try to set the value of a key to a non-string value it will use the JavaScript default toString method, so an object will just be replaced with [object object].

Additionally you can treat localStorage as a regular object and use square bracket notation:

```
var bird = localStorage['birdname'];
```

```
localStorage['birdname'] = 'Gull';
```

Removing items is as simple as calling localStorage.removeItem('key'). If the key you specify doesn't exist, removeItem will conveniently do nothing.

In addition to storing specific information, localStorage is a great tool for caching. In this next section, we'll use the Flickr API to fetch a random photo for Birds of California, and use localStorage as a transparent caching layer to greatly improve the performance of the random image picker on future page loads.

USING WEB STORAGE AS A CACHING LAYER

For the Birds of California site, we can make things a little more exciting for users by incorporating a random image from Flickr, rather than a predefined image. This will sacrifice some of the gains we made in the last chapter in trimming images down to size, in exchange for developer convenience.

We'll use the Flickr search API to find Creative Commons–licensed photos of birds. **Listing 4.1** is a simple JavaScript Flickr API module that uses JSONP to fetch data. For the sake of brevity the code is not included here, but it's available for download from the website. Let's use this module to grab some images related to the California Gull.

LISTING 4.1 Fetching the Flickr data

```
//a couple of convenience functions
var $ = function(selector) {
  return document.querySelector(selector);
};


var getEl = function(id) {
  return document.getElementById(id);
};



var flickr = new Flickr(apikey);
var photoList;

flickr.makeRequest(
  'flickr.photos.search',

  {
    text:'Larus californicus',
    extras:'url_z,owner_name',
    license:5,
    per_page:50
  },

  function(data) {
    photoList = data.photos.photo;
    updatePhoto();
  }
);
```

As you can see, the API takes a method (flickr.photos.search) and some parameters. This will hopefully give us back as many as 50 photos of *Larus Californicus*.

In **Listing 4.2**, the updatePhoto function takes the list, grabs a random photo from the list, and updates the image, the links, and the attribution.

LISTING 4.2 Updating the photo

```
function updatePhoto() {
    var heroImg = document.querySelector('.hero-img');

    //shorthand for "random member of this array"
    var thisPhoto = photoList[Math.floor(Math.random() * photoList.length)];
    $('.hero-img').style.backgroundImage
            = 'url('+ thisPhoto.url_z + ')';

    //update the link
    getEl('imglink').href =
       'http://www.flickr.com/photos/' +
       thisPhoto.owner +
       '/'+ thisPhoto.id;

    //update attribution
    var attr = getEl('attribution');
    attr.href = 'http://www.flickr.com/photos/'
          + thisPhoto.owner;

    attr.innerHTML = thisPhoto.ownername;

}
```

Add this script (with the Flickr API module) to the Birds of California page with a valid Flickr API key and the bird hero image will dynamically update to a random option from the search results list. With no changes to the HTML and CSS from before, however, the user will see the original gull photo, and then a moment later it will be replaced with the result from the API. On one hand, this provides a fallback in case of JavaScript failure for the image. But on the other hand, it doesn't look very nice, and we'll go ahead and say the image is an enhancement to the main content, which is the text.

With that in mind, let's create a null or "loading" state for the links and caption, as shown in **Listing 4.3**.

LISTING 4.3 Hero image null state

```
<div class="hero-shot">
  <a id="imglink" href="#">
  <span class="hero-img"></span></a>
  <p class="caption">
    Photo By <a id="attribution" href="#">...</a>
  </p>
</div>
```

While the data is loading the user needs some indication that something's happening, just so she knows things aren't broken. Normally a spinner of some kind is called for, but in this case let's just add the text "loading" and make the image background gray until it's ready:

```
//show the user we are loading something....
var heroImgElement = $('.hero-img');
heroImgElement.style.background = '#ccc';
heroImgElement.innerHTML = '<p>Loading...</p>';


//Then inside updatePhoto I'll remove the loading state:
heroImgElement.innerHTML = '';
```

So, now we have a pretty nice random image, with a loading state (**Figure 4.1**). However, we're making users wait every time they visit for a random image from a list that probably doesn't change that much. Not only that, but having a very up-to-date list of photos isn't all that important because we just want to add variety, not give up-to-the-minute accurate search results. This is a prime candidate for caching.

FIGURE 4.1 The loading state.

If something is cacheable, it's generally best to abstract away the caching, otherwise the main logic of the application will be cluttered with references to the cache, validation checks, and other logic not relevant to the task at hand. For this call we'll create a new object to serve as a data access layer, so that rather than calling the Flickr API object directly, we'll call the data layer, like so:

```
birdData.fetchPhotos('Larus californicus', function(photos) {
    photoList = photos;
    updatePhoto();
});
```

Because all we ever want to do is search for photos and get back a list, we can hide the Flickr-specific stuff inside this new API. Not only that, but by creating a clean API we can, in theory, change the data source later. If we decide that a different API produces better photo results, we can change the data layer without making changes to any consumers. In this case the key feature is caching. We want to cache API results locally for one day, so that the next time the user visits she'll still get a random photo, but she won't have to wait for a response from the Flickr API.

CREATING THE CACHING LAYER

The fetchPhotos method will first check if this search is cached, and whether the cached data is still valid. If the cache is available and valid, it will return the cached data, otherwise it will make a request to the API and then populate the cache after firing the callback.

First, we'll set up a few variables, as shown in **Listing 4.4**.

LISTING 4.4 A caching layer

```
window.birdData = {};

var memoryCache = {};

var CACHE_TTL = 86400000; //one day in seconds
var CACHE_PREFIX = 'ti';
```

The memoryCache object is a place to cache things fetched from localStorage, so if those items are requested again in the same session they can be returned even faster; fetching data from localStorage is much slower than simply getting data from memory, without including the added cost of decoding a JSON string (remember, localStorage can only store strings). We'll talk more about CACHE_PREFIX and CACHE_TTL shortly.

The first thing we need is a method to write values into cache. We'll cache the response from the Flickr search, but wrap the cached value inside a different object so we can store a timestamp for a cache so that it can be expired.

```
function setCache(mykey, data) {

  var stamp, obj;

  stamp = Date.now();

  obj = {
    date: stamp,
    data: data
  };

  localStorage.setItem(CACHE_PREFIX + mykey, JSON.stringify(obj));
  memoryCache[mykey] = obj;
}
```

We're using CACHE_PREFIX for each of the keys to eliminate the already small chance of collisions. It's possible that another developer on the Birds of California site might decide to use localStorage, so just to be on the safe side we'll prefix our keys. The date value contains a timestamp in seconds, which we can use later to check if the cache has expired. We'll also add the value to the memory cache for quicker access to it if it's fetched again during the same session. We'll use the "setItem" notation for localStorage; this is much clearer than bracket notation—another developer will see right away what is happening, rather than thinking that this is a regular object.

The next function is getCached, which returns the cached data if it's available and valid, or false if the cache is not present or expired (the caller really doesn't need to know which):

```
//fetch cached date if available,
//returns false if not (stale date is treated as unavailable)
function getCached(mykey) {

  var key, obj;

  //prefixed keys to prevent
  //collisions in localStorage, not likely, but
  //a good practice
  key = CACHE_PREFIX + mykey;

  if(memoryCache[key]) {

    if(memoryCache[key].date - Date.now() > CACHE_TTL) {
      return false;
    }
```

```
      return memoryCache[key].data;
  }

  obj = localStorage.getItem(key);

  if(obj) {
      obj = JSON.parse(obj);

      if (Date.now() - obj.date > CACHE_TTL) {
          //cache is expired! let us purge that item
          localStorage.removeItem(key);
          delete(memoryCache[key]);
          return false;
      }
      memoryCache[key] = obj;
      return obj.data;
  }
}
```

This function checks the cache in layers. It starts with the memory cache, because this is the fastest. Then it falls back to localStorage. If it finds the value in localStorage, then it makes sure to also put that value into the memoryCache before returning the data. If no cached value is found, or one of the cached values has expired, then the function returns false.

Next up is the actual fetchPhotos function that encapsulates the caching. All it has to do now is fetch the cached value for the query. If that value is false, then it executes the API method and caches the response. If it is true, then the callback function is called immediately with the cached value.

```
// function to fetch CC flickr photos,
// given a search query. Results are cached for
// one day
function fetchPhotos(query, callback) {
   var flickr, cached;

   cached = getCached(query);

   if(cached) {
      callback(cached.photos.photo);
   } else {

      flickr = new Flickr(API_KEY);
```

```
        flickr.makeRequest(
          'flickr.photos.search',

          {text:query,
           extras:'url_z,owner_name',
           license:5,
           per_page:50},

          function(data) {
            callback(data.photos.photo);

            //set the cache after the
            //callback, so that it happens after
              //any UI updates that may be needed
            setCache(query, data);
          }
        );
      }


    }

    window.birdData.fetchPhotos = fetchPhotos;
```

Now the data call is fully cacheable, with a simple API.

MANAGING LOCALSTORAGE

This is just the beginning for localStorage. Unlike the browser cache, localStorage gives you full manual control. You can decide what to put in, when to take it out, and when to expire it. Some websites (like Google) have actually used localStorage to cache JavaScript and CSS explicitly. It's a powerful tool, so powerful that 5 MB starts to feel a little small sometimes. What do you do when the cache is full? How do you know if the cache is full?

First of all, we can treat localStorage as a normal JavaScript object, so JSON.stringify (localStorage) will return a JSON representation of localStorage. Then we can apply an old trick to figure out how many bytes that uses, including UTF-8 multi-byte characters: unescape(encodeURIComponent('string')).length, which gives us the size of string in bytes. We know that 5 MB is 1024 * 1024 * 5 bytes, so the available space can be found with this:

```
1024 * 1024 * 5 - unescape(encodeURIComponent(JSON.stringify(localStorage))).
  length
```

If you want to know if you've run out of space, WebKit browsers, Opera mobile and Internet Explorer 10 for Windows Phone 8 will throw an exception if you've exceeded the available storage space; if you're worried, you can wrap your setItem call in a try/catch block. When you've run out of storage you can either clear all the values your app has written with localStorage.clear, or keep a separate list in localStorage of all the data you cache and intelligently clear out old values.

THE APPLICATION CACHE

The traditional browser cache, as mentioned previously in this chapter, isn't particularly reliable on mobile. On the other hand, the HTML5 application cache is very reliable on mobile—maybe even too reliable.

WHAT IS THE APPLICATION CACHE?

With features like `localStorage`, you can easily see how a web application could continue to be useful even when not connected to the network. The application cache is designed for that use case.

The idea is to provide a list of all the resources your app needs to function up front, so that the browser can download and cache them. This list is called the manifest. The manifest is identified with a parameter to the <html> tag:

```
<!DOCTYPE html>
<html manifest="birds.appcache">
<head>
```

This file *must* be served with the mime-type `text/cache-manifest`. If it's not, it will be ignored. If you can't configure a custom mime type on your server, you can't use the application cache.

The manifest contains four types of entries:

- MASTER
- CACHE
- NETWORK
- FALLBACK

MASTER

MASTER entries are the files that reference the manifest in their HTML. By including a manifest, these files are implicitly adding themselves to the list. The rest of the entries are included in the manifest file.

CACHE

The CACHE entries define what to cache. Anything in this list *will be* downloaded the first time a visitor comes to the page. The entries will then be cached forever, or until the manifest (not the resource in question) changes.

NETWORK

Because the application cache is designed for offline use, network access actually has to be whitelisted. That means that if a network resource is not listed under network it will be blocked, even if the user is online. For example, if the site includes a Facebook "like" widget inside an iframe, if http://www.facebook.com is not listed in the NETWORK entry, *that iframe will not load.* To allow all network requests you can use the '*' wildcard character.

FALLBACK

These entries allow you to specify fallback content if the user is not online. Entries here are listed as pairs of URLs: the first is the resource requested, the second is the fallback. You have to use relative paths, and everything listed here has to be on the same domain. For example, if you serve images from a CDN on a separate domain you can't define a fallback for that.

CREATING THE CACHE MANIFEST

Here's a manifest for the Birds of California site from the previous chapter:

```
CACHE MANIFEST

# Timestamp:
# 2013-03-15r1

CACHE:
jquery-1.8.0.min.js
gull-360x112.jpg
gull-640x360.jpg
gull-720x225.jpg

FALLBACK:

NETWORK:
*
```

Notice that there are entries for all the different images. Because these are explicit, the browser will download and cache all of them on the first visit to the page, but will never again need to fetch them.

PITFALLS OF THE APPLICATION CACHE

The application cache is the nuclear option. That's because the files in here will *never* expire until the manifest file itself changes, the user clears the cache, or the cache is updated via JavaScript (more on that later). That's why we included a timestamp in the manifest so we can easily force a change to the file if we want to invalidate cached versions in the wild.

The application cache is also completely separate from the browser cache. For example, it is possible to create an application cache that will never revalidate. If you set a far-future Expires header on the manifest file, the browser will cache that file forever. When the application cache checks whether it has changed, it will get the version in the browser cache, see that it is unchanged, and then hold on to the cached files forever (or until the user explicitly clears her cache).

Once the page is cached, it's possible to visit Birds of California without network connectivity. On iOS, offline is guaranteed to work only if the user has bookmarked the page on her home screen. In iOS Safari the contents of the application cache may be evicted if the browser needs to reclaim the space for the browser cache. The cache will still be used.

One of the other pitfalls of the application cache is that once it expires it won't be updated until the next time the user visits. So if a user comes to your site with a stale cache, she'll still see the cached version, even though it's been updated. To make sure users get the latest and greatest bird info, we'll take advantage of the application cache JavaScript API to programmatically check for a stale cache.

AVOIDING A STALE CACHE WITH JAVASCRIPT

The API for the cache hangs off the `window.applicationCache` object. The most important property there is "status." As shown in **Table 4.2**, it has an integer value that represents the current state of the application cache.

TABLE 4.2 Application Cache Status Codes

CODE	NAME	DESCRIPTION
0	UNCACHED	The cache isn't being used.
1	IDLE	The application cache is not currently being updated.
3	CHECKING	The manifest is being downloaded and updates are being made, if available.
4	UPDATEREADY	The new cache is downloaded and ready to use.
5	OBSOLETE	The current cache is stale and cannot be used.

Thankfully, you don't have to remember these numbers; there are constants on the applicationCache object that keep track of the association:

```
> console.log(window.applicationCache.CHECKING)
  2
```

On the Birds of California site, we'll add a short script to check the cache every time the page loads:

```
//alias for convenience
var appCache = window.applicationCache;


appCache.update();
```

This goes at the bottom of page and doesn't need to be ready for the window onload event to do its stuff. At this point we could start polling appCache.status to see if a new version is loaded. When it's calling the swapCache method, it will force the browser to update the changed files in the cache (it will not change what the user is seeing; a reload is still required). It's simpler to use the built-in events that the applicationCache object provides. We can add an event handler to automatically reload the page when the cache is refreshed:

```
var appCache = window.applicationCache;


appCache.addEventListener('updateready', function(e) {


    //let's be defensive and double check the status
    if (appCache.status == appCache.UPDATEREADY) {


        //swap in the new cache!
        appCache.swapCache();


        //Reload the page
        window.location.reload();


    }


});


appCache.update();
```

In addition to the extremely useful "updateready" event, there's a bigger set of events available on the applicationCache object, one for each state we already saw in the status property.

Having the page automatically reload, particularly when the user is in the middle of looking at the site, is a terrible user experience. There are several ways to handle this. Using a confirm dialog box or whisper tip to ask the user to reload to fetch new content is better, but still not great. In the next chapter we'll explore a much better way to handle this, and other cases, by dynamically updating the content with AJAX.

THE 404 PROBLEM

If any of the resources in the CACHE entry can't be retrieved when the browser attempts to fetch them, the browser ignores the cache manifest. This means that if a user visits your site and for some reason one of the requests fails, it will be as if she were a completely new visitor the next time she visits—the cache will be useless. That means the cache is quite brittle: unless all the requests are successful, there's no caching at all—it's all or nothing.

THE APPLICATION CACHE: WORTH THE PAIN?

The application cache is obviously fraught with difficulties, not the least of which is how difficult it is to invalidate. It gives you a lot of power, but at the cost of flexibility and maintainability. Users love an app that launches instantly, but everyone hates strange errors. The stickiness of the application cache leads necessarily to strange bugs that are hard to chase down. When you use it, you'll eventually end up with a file that you just can't seem to get out of cache. It isn't that the application cache is buggy; it's that it's completely unforgiving. If you deploy a bad cache, it can be a real problem to undo the error.

Optimizing for browser cache and using the much more flexible web storage API is usually a better choice, but when you want the fastest possible launch time, and you're willing to accept the difficulties, the application cache is an incredible tool.

WRAPPING UP

Caching is one of the most powerful tools for optimizing performance. It's one of the basics that you really want to get right before you move on to more complex optimizations. In this chapter we covered the fundamentals of the browser cache and some simple optimization strategies. We discussed web storage and using it for caching data. Finally we talked about the application cache, which is powerful, if a bit finicky.

In the next chapter we'll look at how to work around the overhead of page loads entirely with PJAX.

FURTHER READING

The complete APIs for web storage and the application cache are well covered on the Mozilla Developer Network:

- https://developer.mozilla.org/en-US/docs/DOM/Storage
- https://developer.mozilla.org/en-US/docs/HTML/Using_the_application_cache

CHAPTER 5

Using PJAX to Improve the Touch Experience

So far, this book has focused on page loads, and with good reason—page loads are the slowest part of the web experience. On touch devices with high-latency connections even the most optimized page loads can still be painfully slow.

It might not be so bad if page loads happened only once, but most websites have more than one page. Navigating between pages is one of the biggest pain points for users, but page load times can be improved only so much. This chapter describes how you can avoid page loads altogether to dramatically speed up the user experience.

THE PRICE OF PAGE LOADS

To start with let's take the example from the previous chapter, with the randomized image, and make the initial page load as fast as possible. We'll add all three scripts inline onto the page to limit the cost of the additional requests, minify the JavaScript code with Closure Compiler (to reduce byte count), and make sure all the headers are optimized.

We'll do some profiling on the page, to get a sense of what's still slow after the Flickr API request is cached. **Figure 5.1** shows where the time is spent.

FIGURE 5.1 Time spent during a page load.

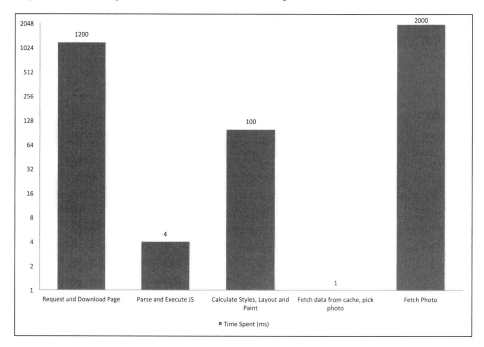

If the customer told me this site was slow he'd be right: going from one bird page to another takes a second and a half! Looking at the graph, we know we can't do too much about how fast a photo is downloaded from Flickr. Because it's a random photo we can't really optimize there. But the first three bars on the graph make up a lot of the time and they're all consequences of loading a new page. Optimizing the first load will make these bars as short as they can get. The next step will be to do away with page loads altogether using PJAX, which refers to the combination of pushState and AJAX: AJAX to update the content, and pushState to update the URL.

WHY NOT JUST USE AJAX?

If we look back at the page, it's clear that only a small amount of the page is actually changing between page loads (**Figure 5.2**).

FIGURE 5.2 The page changes only slightly between loads.

FIGURE 5.3 Sharing a link via built-in Twitter.

So let's change only that part of the page. To do this, we can simply make an AJAX request that returns just the piece of HTML changes, then insert that into the DOM. This would work great, but it would actually hurt the usability of the site.

Listing 5.1 shows the navigation HTML.

LISTING 5.1 The Birds of California navigation HTML

```
<ul class="bird-list">
  <li class="nav-li">
    <a class="nav-link" href="california_condor.html">California Condor</a>
  </li>
  <li class="nav-li">
    <a class="nav-link" href="california_quail.html">California Quail</a>
  </li>
  <li class="nav-li">
    <a class="nav-link" href="california_gull.html">California Gull</a>
  </li>
</ul>
```

The structure couldn't be cleaner. Each bird has its own HTML file. The URLs for these files are actually an important part of the interface. A user can navigate the site just by guessing links; the pattern is simple, so next time the user's on the bus and wants to look up a specific bird on his phone he can just type domain/california_gull.html and probably get to the right page. On touch devices there's another important factor: the touch operating systems all have built-in sharing. The user might see a cool bird, then tap the Share button and tweet a link to the bird he's seeing (**Figure 5.3**).

When the user's followers see the link, they can click it and see the exact content shown in the little thumbnail. All of this seems pretty obvious, of course, but when developers start thinking about how much benefit they can gain from using JavaScript and AJAX to update their page content, they lose touch with some of the web's most basic user interface conventions.

None of these conventions are more basic than the URL. Most web users know what a URL is and understand that it points to a specific "thing" on the Internet. When they click a link from Twitter they fully expect the content they see to be the same that their friend saw. Breaking links is a big mistake. If we just changed this page to use JavaScript to change the bird when the user tapped on one of the links we would break all the URLs. That's why we have to use the HTML5 browser history API. Not because it's cool (although it is), but because preserving links is critical.

THE BROWSER HISTORY API

There's been a `history` object in the window namespace for a long time. The browser history is a large stack that stores the user's session history in a tab; it's what makes the Back button work. Think of the browser history like a stack of cards, with each card representing a URL the user has visited.

UNDERSTANDING BROWSER HISTORY

As the user navigates the site, he adds cards, or states, to his history. When he clicks the Back button, he moves back one card, and when he clicks the Forward button, he advances one card. When he copies the URL or uses a browser Share button, he takes a snapshot of where he is, without the cards in front or behind. The URL is a reference to the state in the stack, which ultimately maps to one resource (**Figure 5.4**).

FIGURE 5.4
The browser history as a stack of cards.

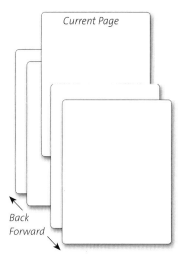

The browser history API gives us two new methods to manipulate this stack: pushState and replaceState. pushState lets us add a new card to the front of the stack, removing any cards in front. This is pretty much the same thing that happens when a user clicks a link: he gets a new state entry, and if he were in the middle of the history stack anything further forward is lost. replaceState lets us replace the current card without impacting the rest of the stack.

With pushState alone, we can make sure that links the user shares or bookmarks properly reflect the state of the page. We can't handle the Back or Forward buttons; in fact, when we use pushState, the Back button doesn't trigger a page load until the user goes back far enough to where the states weren't added with pushState. For this purpose, the browser history API provides an event called popstate that fires when the position in the state stack has been changed by the user using the Back or Forward buttons.

CHANGING HISTORY WITH PUSHSTATE

Let's give it a try. For the "hello world" of pushState, we'll create a simple little interface.

> **NOTE:** See the Listing 5.2 file on the companion book site for the complete code.

```
<h1 id="number">1</h1>
<a id="forward" href="?"num=2>Go forward!</a>
```

The idea is that when you click or tap on Go Forward the number increases in increments, and the URL updates with a query parameter num with the value of the number.

First we'll add a click handler to the forward link:

```
var link = document.getElementById('forward');
var num = document.getElementById('number');

link.addEventListener('click', function(e) {
    e.preventDefault();
    var myNum = parseInt(num.innerHTML, 10); // it is always a good idea to
    → make sure the type is correct
    num.innerHTML = ++myNum;
});
```

Now when you click the link the number goes up. But we want the URL to update so that when we click the Back button the number goes back down. First, let's use pushState:

> **NOTE:** See the Listing 5.3 file on the companion book site for the complete code.

```
link.addEventListener('click', function(e) {
   e.preventDefault();
   var myNum = parseInt(num.innerHTML, 10);
   num.innerHTML = ++myNum;
   history.pushState({count:myNum}, null, '?num=' + myNum);
   document.title = 'Number ' + myNum;
});
```

The pushState method takes three parameters:

- An object representing the "state"
- A title
- A URL

The title parameter is not the window title, which must be updated separately. At the moment none of the major mobile browsers do anything with the title parameter, but there's no guarantee they won't some time in the future. To be on the safe side, we'll just pass null.

HANDLING THE POPSTATE EVENT

If you try this code in the browser you'll see the URL and title updating as the number increases. The Back button, however, will have no effect. To handle the Back button, let's add a listener to the popstate event:

NOTE: See the Listing 5.4 file on the companion book site for the complete code.

```
addEventListener('popstate', function(e) {
   if( e.state && e.state.count ) {
      num.innerHTML = e.state.count;
      document.title = 'Number ' + e.state.count;
   } else {
      setNumFromUrl()
   }
});
```

Because we passed the count inside the state object, we can actually use this value from the popstate event. We need to test for the value though, because popstate fires on page-Load as well, and on pageLoad the state property of the event will be null. We'll also add another function: setNumFromUrl. Because there's no server code for this little demo, we need to make sure that the links to specific numbers, which will no doubt be shared far and wide, actually show the number the user was looking at.

That function isn't fancy, but it's necessary; we have to guarantee that the URL actually reflects what the user sees. We can't break user expectations.

> **NOTE:** See the Listing 5.4 file on the companion book site for the complete code.

```
function setNumFromUrl() {
    if(location.search) {
        var match = location.search.match(/num=([0-9]+)/);
        if(match) {
            document.getElementById('number').innerHTML = match[1];
            document.title = 'Number ' + match[1];
        }
    } else {
        document.getElementById('number').innerHTML = 1;
        document.title = 'Number 1';
    }
}
```

Now the document will always show the correct number, and if no number is specified, it will show number 1. Now you can load the page, increment the number, and then navigate forward and backward. And when you inevitably tweet this URL to share it with your friends, they'll see the same number you did.

PUSHSTATE BROWSER SUPPORT AND FALLBACKS

pushState works great in most mobile browsers, but not all of them. Most importantly, the Android default browser doesn't support it in versions 3.0 and up. (It works fine in 2.2–3.) Chrome for Android supports it properly, but Chrome isn't the default in phones without Android 4.1 ("Jelly Bean") pre-installed. So as wonderful as pushState is we need to fall back for browsers that don't have it.

TABLE 5.1 pushState browser support

PLATFORM	BROWSER HISTORY API SUPPORT
iOS	4.2–4.3[*], 5.0+
Android	2.2, 2.3, 4.0.4[*]
Chrome for Android	All versions
Internet Explorer	10+ (Windows Phone 8)

[*] iOS 4 and Android 4 partially support browser history. popstate is fired, reload will reload with the correct URL, and share actions will share the URL set via pushState, but the UI will not update the URL.

It's easy to detect if pushState is supported: `window.history` won't have the pushState method if it isn't supported. (On iOS 4 and Android, pushState works well enough for our purposes, bugs aside.) But how do you provide a fallback? You still need to update the URL and you still need users to be able to share links. One recommendation is to fall back to update the `location.hash`. This is the value after # in a URL. Changing this value creates a history entry, and by continuously checking the URL it is possible to simulate the popstate event.

Going back to the last example, we'll add feature detection for pushState. If pushState is unavailable, we'll fall back to using `location.hash`. For users with browsers that don't support pushState, the URL will look like this:

`history.html#4`

rather than

`history.html?num=4`

The simple feature detection code looks like this:

NOTE: See the Listing 5.5 file on the companion book site for the complete code.

```
var useHash = false;
var hashExp = /#([0-9]+)/;
if(!history.pushState) {
   useHash = true;
}
useHash = true;
```

Next we'll consolidate all the code that updates the HTML into the `handleStateChange` function. This code also updates the href for the link, so that copying and pasting that link will work properly:

NOTE: See the Listing 5.6 file on the companion book site for the complete code.

```
function handleStateChange(count) {
   num.innerHTML = count;
   document.title = 'Number ' + count;
   link.href = '?num=' + (parseInt(count,10) + 1);
}
```

Then, we'll update the `setNumFromUrl` function to support both the query string and the hash URL.

UPGRADING AND DOWNGRADING URLS

At this point we have a bit of a problem: users who come to the site with shared deep links will end up with a strange experience. If an Android 3 user loads `history.html?num=2` and then taps "Go forward," the URL will become `history.html?num=2#3`, which doesn't make sense. If an iOS 6 user loads `history.html#2` and then clicks "Go forward," his first history entry will be the fallback URL, and then following entries will be correct.

We want the experience to be consistent. So if a user loads `history.html?num=2` but his browser doesn't support push state, we'll reload the page with the fallback version, to keep URLs consistent. This isn't a great experience for the user, but without pushState it's either that or accept inconsistent URLs.

On the other hand, if a user comes to the site with a hash URL, we can *upgrade* the URL to the non-hash URL rather than the fallback. We could use `pushState`, but that would create a history entry. In this case `replaceState` is the right tool for the job, because we can change the state without adding a history entry.

Listing 5.7 shows the new, expanded function, with upgrading and downgrading.

LISTING 5.7 Handling and upgrading incoming links

```
function setNumFromUrl() {

  //There is a query string, so handle that
  if(location.search) {

    var match = location.search.match(/num=([0-9]+)/);
    if(match) {

      //if pushState doesn't work, we need to
      //scrub the query string and redirect to the hash version
      if(useHash) {
        location = 'history.html#' + match[1];

      } else {
        document.getElementById('number').innerHTML = match[1];
        document.title = 'Number ' + match[1];
      }
    }

  //No query string, but there is a hash, so we should use that
  }else if (location.hash) {

    var match = location.hash.match(hashExp);
```

```
      document.getElementById('number').innerHTML = match[1];
      document.title = 'Number ' + location.hash;

      //if the user can use push state, but came with a hash url,
      //we can upgrade the url with replaceState.
      if(!useHash) {
        history.replaceState({count:match[1]}, null, '
              history.html?num=' + match[1]);
      }

    //The default state
    } else {
      document.getElementById('number').innerHTML = 1;
      document.title = 'Number 1';
    }
}
```

This function could be improved with more validation to make sure it doesn't break when invalid values are added to the hash, but for our purposes this illustrates the idea. As stated before, for user agents that don't support pushState we'll need to continuously check the URL for changes in case the user clicks the Back button. To reduce overhead we want to do this only when necessary. See **Listing 5.8**.

LISTING 5.8 A cross-browser URL state change handler

```
//consolidate the update into one place
function handleStateChange(count) {
   num.innerHTML = count;
   document.title = 'Number ' + count;
}

if(!useHash) {

   //this is the lightweight bversion
   addEventListener('popstate', function(e) {
      if( e.state && e.state.count ) {
         handleStateChange(e.state.count);
      } else {
         setNumFromUrl();
      }
   });
```

```
} else {
    //because the first popstate isn't called,
    //we need to call this manually
    setNumFromUrl();

    //we need to know the old value
    //to be able to see if it changed
    var oldHash = location.hash;

    //poll every 100ms
    window.setInterval(function(){
        var match;
        if( window.hash !== oldHash ){
            match = location.hash.match(hashExp);
            oldHash = location.hash;
            if(match) {
                handleStateChange(match[1]);
            }
        }
    }, 100);
}
```

Now this code is nice and resilient. It works with—and *without*—pushState. With a little effort on the server I could also make sure this works with JavaScript disabled as well, creating a fast experience with no refresh that still works as the user might expect.

THE HASH-BANG

In your travels across the web you may have encountered URLs that look like this: mysite.com/#!news/world/123. This is what has come to be known as a *hash-bang url*. (Hash and bang are Unix speak for "#" and "!" respectively.) These URLs are doing what our simple fragment was doing: making sure a single-page app works on browsers that don't support the history API. The weird syntax was proposed by Google, allowing the Googlebot to index content that is loaded only via AJAX.

The browser history API makes hash-bang URLs obsolete; rather than a hack to preserve history, you can now provide real URLs that represent your pages. Don't use hash-bang URLs. The simple site described in this chapter is designed to work with any URL typed directly into the address bar. The # URLs are a fallback that the Googlebot doesn't need to know about. Rather than use a hack to support SEO, it is possible and preferable to make sure your site works with proper URLs.

ADDING PJAX

pushState is an amazing tool that can drastically improve the perceived performance of your site by enabling PJAX. If you recall, PJAX is pushState plus AJAX. With both together we can update just a piece of the page and the URL, dramatically speeding up the site.

USING HTML FRAGMENTS

As previously shown in this chapter, the different bird pages on the site really aren't all that different. Probably about 10 percent of the bytes on the page are actually changing when the user taps on a different bird. We'll make some changes so that when the user taps on a different bird the content and the URL will update, but the page won't actually reload. For the purposes of this book the site will not work without JavaScript, but in production you should replicate this logic on the server so that a user going directly to california_condor.html will see the same page, even if JavaScript is disabled.

We'll create HTML fragments for the different birds, to save download time. When the user taps on a bird he just needs to download these tiny fragments, rather than the whole page:

```
california_condor_frag.html
california_gull_frag.html
california_quail_frag.html
```

For example, california_condor_frag.html looks like this:

```
<p>The California Condor (<i>Gymnogyps californianus</i>) is a large vulture.
    In fact, it is the largest land bird in North America. Aside from its size
    the condor is probably best know for its rarity: there are only 226 birds
    living in the wild, which is up from 22 in 1987</p>
<p>The bird is black, except for patches of white under the wings and its bald,
    red head.</p>
```

That's it. Just the minimum, but containing rendered HTML. Next we'll create a "wrapper" file that includes the same boilerplate that every page needs. That includes the JavaScript and CSS, as well as the rest of the HTML outside of the <section class="content">, just as we did it in the last chapter. Because this page will be loaded only once per session, caching JavaScript and CSS files will be even less useful than normal, so we'll seriously optimize for the first load. That means putting all the JavaScript and CSS inline on the page, fully minimized. (See the website for the complete file.) With all the JavaScript, CSS, and HTML this ends up squishing down to a tiny 2.8 KB zipped. The first load shouldn't be too bad, but subsequent loads will be the real benefit.

Before we go farther let's set a baseline. Loading this page, even with optimizations, takes about 1.2 seconds over 3G, not including the image. Including the image (with the Flickr data cached), it takes 2.3 seconds. That's the best we can do with normal page loads. After we build a single-page version we'll come back to this number.

CREATING A ROUTER

There are many ways to build a single-page app. The cleanest approach is to use a "router." A router works a bit like a router in a server-side framework. It takes URLs and then calls to the proper code to handle that URL.

With the code in one place, URLs can be passed to the router from clicks intercepted on anchors in the page, or from pushState events. For the Birds of California site we'll make a dead simple router. It has two methods: addRoute and handleRoute. The addRoute method takes a regular expression representing a URL, a callback, and a scope object. The handleRoute method simply takes a URL.

We'll implement it as a simple stack. Adding a route pushes information about that route on to the stack. When a path is routed we simply loop through all the routes until we find one that matches, and then dispatch to that one. See **Listing 5.9**.

LISTING 5.9 The router

```
var routes = [];

//this will push the new route onto the
//list of routes.
function addRoute(route, callback, scope){

    //create a consistent signature that
    //we can rely on later
    var routeObj = {
      route: route,
      callback: callback,
      scope: scope
    };

    routes.push(routeObj);
}

//looks for matching routes, then calls the callback
function handleRoute(path, noHistory) {

  var len = routes.length, scope;

  for (var i=0; i < len; i++) {
    if(path.match(routes[i].route)) {

        //if the caller provided a scope,
```

```
            //we use it, otherwise we will execute
            //the callback in the window scope
            if(routes[i].scope) {
               scope = routes[i].scope;
            } else {
               scope = window;
            }

            // if this is from a popstate,
            // we shouldn't push state again
            if(!noHistory) {
               //push the path onto the history stack
               history.pushState({}, null, path);
            }

            routes[i].callback.apply(scope, [path]);
            return true;
         }
      }
      //no route found, move on
      return false;
}
```

In the addRoute method we've provided a way to pass a scope object. When the callback is called this object will become "this" inside that function. Providing the ability to pass a scope with a callback makes things a little more convenient for someone calling the API.

For addRoute the scope is optional. If it isn't present, we'll execute the callback in the window scope, to avoid any scope confusion later. The nice thing about this router is that all we have to do to get history to work is add a listener:

```
window.addEventListener('popstate', function(e) {
   handleRoute(window.location.href, true);
})
window.router = {
   handleRoute:handleRoute,
   addRoute: addRoute
};
```

Now history is managed automatically, assuming that all the code on the page is executed via a route. The AJAX part of the PJAX should look pretty familiar. The code for a very simple AJAX module to handle the actual request is available on the website, but you should use one of the many frameworks out there; this code is very limited. The idea now is to intercept all the clicks on the page, see if they have a defined route, and then execute that route. The router defined in Listing 5.9 returns `true` if a route is found, `false` if not.

INTERCEPTING EVENTS

For the router to work properly we need to catch every click on the page to test and then intercept them. To do this we'll add an event listener on the `document` element. Because click events bubble up the DOM tree, adding a click listener to the `document` element makes sure we catch them all. See **Listing 5.10**.

LISTING 5.10 Intercepting clicks

```
//intercept all the clicks, if they are on anchors
//pass them to the router.
document.addEventListener('click', function(e) {

    //if it has an href, assume it is an anchor
    if(e.target.href) {
        if(router.handleRoute(e.target.href)) {
            e.preventDefault();
        }
    }

}, true);
```

IMPLEMENTING A ROUTE

Then we add a route, as shown in **Listing 5.11**.

LISTING 5.11 A route implementation

```
//build up data for routes, so we don't
//have to keep looking up Latin names
var latinNameMap = {};
var links = document.querySelectorAll('.nav-link');
var href;

//cache the ajax responses in memory,
//so next time the user goes to that bird
//it's faster
var pageCache = {};
```

```
//rather than lookup each time, we'll
//grab all the Latin names and cache them at init time
for (var i=0, len = links.length; i < len; i++) {
   href = normalizeLink(links[i].href);
   latinNameMap[href] = links[i].getAttribute('data-latin');
}

//browsers behave differently with links, and what they
//include, even for relative paths.
function normalizeLink(path) {
   return path.match(/([a-z_]+\.html)/)[1];
}

//this function handles the route callbacks
function handlePage(path) {
   var href = normalizeLink(path);
   birdData.changePhoto(latinNameMap[href]);

   if(pageCache[href]) {
      document.querySelector('.content').innerHTML = pageCache[href];
   } else {
      ajax.makeRequest(href.replace('.html', '_frag.html'), function(xhr) {
         document.querySelector('.content').innerHTML = xhr.responseText;
         pageCache[href] = xhr.responseText;

      }, this);
   }
}

router.addRoute(/[a-z_]+\.html/, handlePage);
```

As you can see, all links and popstate events go through the same code. The handlePage function runs either way so the page behaves the same way. This is how we make the Back button work! We also added a very light caching layer. After the AJAX requests we store the response in an object, then if the user goes back to that path, via a click or the Back button, there's no need to make another request. Remember how this page wouldn't load in less than one second even when fully optimized? Now with PJAX the first page load takes the same amount of time. But the next load—a tap on another bird—takes just 700 ms on 3G. And if the data is cached in memory and the user goes back to a bird he already saw, it takes about 3 ms to change pages. This kind of improvement in performance is why using PJAX, or another single-page approach, is becoming popular.

MAKING THIS EVEN FASTER

Now this approach is pretty fast as it stands. But it has some minor issues, such as the random bird code. It slows things down, and it's a little weird to have the bird change when the user hits the Back button. So we'll save the entire content of the container `<div>` in the DOM, maybe with display hidden, and then swap in new content. With the page as it is that's fairly complex; we need to modify the `birdData` code to create new HTML, rather than just use what's on the page. Also, it's a small thing, but we're sending HTML for our AJAX request. For this example a couple of `<p>` tags isn't too much, but for a more complex fragment the HTML ends up being quite a lot of bytes, and if the pages share a template that's a lot of duplicate bytes. What we need is a template.

For most seasoned web developers, rendering templates on the client sounds a little insane. Luckily modern JavaScript engines have become so fast that rendering templates on the client is actually *faster* than it would be in many server frameworks, and no longer insane at all.

Templating engines generally grow more complex over time. The most mature templating systems, like Smarty or JSP, are languages in their own right. The simplest templating system, however, is as simple as labeling holes in your text that you want to fill with data. For many purposes a templating engine can just be search and replace. For the Birds of California site, we'll do just that. We'll create a data object that represents the content, and a template that indicates what to replace.

We'll include the template on the page inside a script block. If you set the type attribute of the `<script>` tag to something that the browser doesn't recognize it won't attempt to parse it, but you can still access the contents from JavaScript (unlike a comment). For a simple search and replace we can employ a token format used by a few templating engines: keywords surrounded by double braces. Using double braces makes sure that CSS or JavaScript in a template won't cause problems. See **Listing 5.12**.

LISTING 5.12 The bird template

```
<script type="x/template" id="tmpl">
<div class="container main">
    <h2 id="birdname">{{birdname}}</h2>
    <div class="hero-shot">
        <a id="imglink" href="{{imagelink}}">
        <span role="img" aria-label="A bird" class="hero-img"></span></a>
        <p class="caption">
```

```
    Photo By
    <a id="attribution" href="{{authorurl}}">{{author}}</a></p>
  </div>
  <section class="content">
    {{content}}
  </section>
</div>
</script>
```

The template parser will take a template and an object. For each token it finds in the template, it will look in the object passed for members that match the token name. If it finds one, it will replace the token with the value; otherwise it will replace it with the original token for debugging purposes. This is done via an underused feature in JavaScript: `String.prototype.replace` can take a callback as the second argument. We'll use a regular expression to pull out the tokens, then a simple callback function to search the data object for matches.

The regular expression that finds the tokens uses non-capturing groups to find the tokens, and allows only keywords to start with a letter. The keywords are in a capturing group that we can use later. See **Listing 5.13**.

LISTING 5.13 A template renderer

```
var regexp = /(?:\{\{)([a-zA-z][^\s\}]+)(?:\}\})/g

function render(template, data) {

  return template.replace(regexp, function(fullMatch, capture) {
    if(data[capture]) {
      return data[capture];
    } else {
      return fullMatch;
    }
  });
}


window.renderTemplate = render;
```

For simplicity's sake, we'll assume that rather than use our client-side bird randomizer we'll instead use a single, server-side API that gives us the JSON we need for all the data. The plan is to change the route handler so that instead of updating the DOM, it will fetch the data from the new JSON API, render the template, and then insert it into the DOM. See **Listing 5.14**.

LISTING 5.14 API response

```
{
   "birdname" : "California Quail",
   "image_link": "http://www.flickr.com/photos/98528214@N00/290921246",
   "img_url":"http://farm1.staticFlickr.com/117/290921246_e1d0e9e52f_z.jpg",
   "author_url":"http://www.flickr.com/photos/furryscalyman/",
   "author":"furryscaly",
   "content":"<p>The California Quail (<i>Callipepla californica</i>).."
}
```

As an added optimization, we'll create a new element for each page, hiding the others. When the user hits the Back button or clicks a link to a page he's already seen, we'll just show and hide elements, making the page loads as fast as possible.

We'll need a few variables and a new utility function, as shown in **Listing 5.15**.

LISTING 5.15 A hide pages function

```
var pages = {};
var idInc = 0;
var tmpl = document.getElementById('tmpl').innerHTML;

function hidePages() {
   var page;

   for (page in pages) {
      pages[page].style.display = 'none';
   }
}
```

Then, as shown in **Listing 5.16**, we'll modify the handlePage function use the template renderer and JSON API.

LISTING 5.16 A templatized handlePage function

```
//this function handles the route callbacks
function handlePage(path) {
   var href = normalizeLink(path);
   var thispage;

   if(!pages[href]) {

      //hide all the other pages right away
      hidePages();
```

```
ajax.makeRequest(href.replace('.html', '.json'), function(xhr) {
    var data = JSON.parse(xhr.responseText);

    //create an elment to hold the page
    var contentHolder = document.createElement('div');

    //give it an id
    contentHolder.id = 'birds-' + idInc++;

    //and render the template into it
    contentHolder.innerHTML = renderTemplate(tmpl, data);
    document.querySelector('.main').appendChild(contentHolder);

    pages[href] = contentHolder;

  }, this);
} else {
  hidePages();
  pages[href].style.display = 'block';
}
}
```

Now this page should be about as fast as you can imagine it. Pages load instantly when they're already cached—it really is a great experience.

PRUNING

Creating hidden DOM nodes is a great way to speed things up, but over time it can actually slow things down. If the Birds of California site had thousands of bird species, a dedicated birder might view hundreds of pages during a research session. Each page contains some text and an image. All of that is in the DOM, using up memory. As stated before, of all the things in short supply on most touch devices, memory is probably the biggest behind browser cache. Every DOM node requires memory. And every image requires lots of memory. If we just keep creating nodes eventually the browser will slow down and maybe even crash.

A robust system will *prune* nodes as they become less useful. The actual data for the page (rather than the rendered template) is quite small, and can probably be kept around indefinitely. All you have to do when the node has been destroyed is rebuild the node, not actually fetch the data.

The simplest strategy is to set a maximum number of nodes. When you exceed that number, destroy the node that has been hidden the longest, that is, the one that's least frequently used. It's good practice to keep no more than ten hidden nodes at a time, unless they are very simple.

SINGLE-PAGE FRAMEWORKS

In this chapter we built a router, a template renderer, and a cacheable PJAX system. It's actually starting to look a little like a framework. There are a few storm clouds though: the data model is complex and brittle. It's also not very easy to build on. What if the client later decides he wants to show a map of where to find the bird? What if the client wants to create editing tools? When site requirements reach a certain level of complexity developers working on server code turn to the MVC (Model-View-Controller) pattern, and often they turn to frameworks and template engines. You can learn more about MVC in Appendix C, which you can download from touch-interfaces.com.

If you want something more robust for templating than simple search and replace, there are several great choices for client templating, from the very simple (Mustache) to the very complex (EJS). **Table 5.2** shows some of the most popular ones. Take note of which ones support other languages; it can be very useful to share templates between the client and the server.

TABLE 5.2 Client-side templating languages

NAME	AVAILABLE IN OTHER LANGUAGES	WEBSITE
Mustache	PHP, Ruby, Python, Scala, .NET	http://mustache.github.com
Handlebars.js	Only JavaScript	http://handlebarsjs.com
HAML	Ruby	https://github.com/creationix/haml-js
Jade	Only JavaScript (Node)	http://jade-lang.com
Underscore Template	Only JavaScript	http://underscorejs.org
EJS	Only JavaScript	http://embeddedjs.com

WRAPPING UP

For most websites, the biggest pain point for users is waiting for the next page to load. Using the browser history API with AJAX makes it possible to completely eliminate those loads. Additionally, because you control page loads, you can properly message the user that things are loading to keep the interface feeling fast. An added benefit is that users will notice only that things are fast, not that you're doing something odd or different.

In the next chapter we'll look at how to improve interactions with browser events.

CHAPTER 6

Taps vs. Clicks: Basic Event Handling

In 1984, the Macintosh was the first widely adopted platform with a graphic interface. The original Macintosh came with a tour of the interface, which included a little game called Mousing Around to teach users how to use a mouse.

In 2007, when Apple introduced the iPhone, which I would consider the first modern touch device, it didn't include a game explaining how to use the touch interface. Humans understand instinctively how touching something can affect it. With a mouse it takes a while to get used to the idea that moving one thing can effect change on another. With touch, we use skills we've had since we were toddlers.

If the fundamental interaction of a mouse-based interface is the click, the fundamental interaction of a touch interface is the tap. At first, tapping seems like more or less the same thing as a click. In reality a tap is quite different.

WHAT MAKES A TAP DIFFERENT?

On the desktop, when you want to click on a link, you first have to move the cursor over the link, and then click. On a touch interface there's only one movement—when you want to follow a link, you tap it. There's no moving the cursor, no hover event. The click event itself is a combination of mousedown and mouseup. A tap is a single discreet event, defined only as the user touching the screen.

Most importantly, a tap is produced by physically touching the device, rather than pressing a button on a separate device. This is not a trivial difference. If you've used a MacBook, you've experienced Apple's trackpads that have no physical buttons. Nevertheless, when you press the trackpad to click, the trackpad itself makes a clicking sound. That clicking sound is the feedback to tell you that your touch worked. When you touch the screen of a touch device, there's no real physical response (some Android devices vibrate slightly). A good touch interface gives you immediate feedback. On the home screen of the iPhone, touching one of the icons causes it to highlight immediately, even though there's a slight delay before the app launches. If you didn't have that immediate feedback, the iPhone would feel significantly slower: the visceral feeling of lag on touch comes from a delay between when you touch the device and when it responds. Because a touch device doesn't have buttons, tap interactions themselves are overloaded. Instead of a right click, there's "tap and hold." For zoom, most devices have implemented a "double tap." Tap twice on the screen and it will zoom in (even if you tap on a link or an element with an onclick handler). Because of this overloading, the browser will actually wait around 300 milliseconds before firing an onclick handler, just to make sure that the event isn't the beginning of a double tap.

If you think back to Chapter 2, "Creating a Simple Content Site," 300 milliseconds is an eternity. Adding that much time to your page load would be like moving your server 55,000 miles away. This is the reason the quiz from the last chapter seemed a little slow. It *was* a little slow, because each click was delayed by 300 milliseconds. To get the best performance out of a touch interface you need to turn to touch events rather than click events.

INTRODUCING TOUCH EVENTS

Even though touch devices don't have mice, their browsers still generate mouse events. onclick, mouseover, mousedown, and mouseup all still happen. On the touch-enabled browser they're not "real" events, they are synthetic. The browser creates the events based on touch behaviors that seem a bit like a mouse event.

A click is generated when a user taps on an element but does not leave his finger on the screen. The onclick event is fired 300ms after the tap. onmouseup and onmousedown are fired the same time as onclick.

The browser fires these events so that websites that don't consider touch still work. If you want to make a good touch interface, skip the synthetic events and go straight to the source and work from touch events.

On mobile browsers there are four types of events related to touch (**Table 6.1**):

- When the touch starts (the user puts his finger on the screen)
- When the touchpoint moves (the user moves his finger without removing it from the screen)
- When the touch ends (the user takes his finger off the screen)
- When a touch is canceled (something, such as a notification, interrupts the touch)

NOTE: WebKit, Opera Mobile, and Firefox mobile all use roughly the same API. Internet Explorer 10 for Windows Phone 8 uses a very different model, which we'll cover shortly.

TABLE 6.1 Touch events in WebKit

EVENT NAME	DESCRIPTION	CONTAINS TOUCHES ARRAY
touchstart	Start of touch	Yes
touchmove	Touchpoint changes	Yes
touchend	Touch ends	Yes
touchcancel	Touch is interrupted	No

The touches array is a group of touch objects generated by a touch event. A touch object represents the finger touching the screen (**Table 6.2**).

TABLE 6.2 Properties of the touch object

PROPERTY	DESCRIPTION
identifier	Unique identifier for this touch. As long as the user keeps her finger on the screen, this will not change.
screenX	The X position of the touch, relative to the left side of the device screen, regardless of scrolling.
screenY	The Y position, relative to the top of the screen.
clientX	The X position relative to the left side of the browser viewport, in subtracting any browser chrome. In general this is the same as screenX.
clientY	The Y position relative to the top of the viewport; the equivalent of screenY minus the browser chrome.
pageX	The X position relative to the left of the rendered page.
pageY	The Y position relative to the top of the rendered page.
target	The element under the touchpoint when the touch started. If the touch moves over a different element, this value does not change.
radius[X/Y]*	The radius of the touchpoint (an estimate of the size of the contact with the screen).
rotationAngle*	The angle of the ellipsis described in radius needs to be rotated to most closely match the touch area.
force*	The force being applied to the surface.

* radius, rotationAngle, and force are prefixed on Chrome for Android (webkitForce) and may not be populated if the device does not provide this information. All three are unsupported as of iOS 6.

INTERNET EXPLORER 10 AND POINTER EVENTS

IE10 theoretically supports the same events. The syntax, however, is completely different. In IE10 Microsoft has tried to generically handle events so the same code can work with both touch and mouse input—IE10 desktop supports the same events as IE10 for tablets and phones.

In IE10 there's a single event called a "pointer" event. Pointer events fire for mouse clicks, stylus taps, and finger touches (**Table 6.3**).

TABLE 6.3 Internet Explorer pointer events

EVENT NAME	DESCRIPTION (ON TOUCH DEVICES)
MSPointerDown	Start of touch
MSPointerMove	Touchpoint moved
MSPointerUp	Touch ends
MSPointerOver	Touchpoint is over the element
MSPointerOut	Touchpoint leaves the element

The event object (MSPointerEvent) extends MouseEvent and contains the page[x|y], client[x|y], and device[x|y] properties. It also contains additional "pointer" properties (**Table 6.4**).

TABLE 6.4 MSPointerEvent properties

PROPERTY	DESCRIPTION
hwTimestamp	The time when the event was created in milliseconds.
isPrimary	Indication of whether or not this pointer is the primary pointer.
pointerId	Unique ID for the pointer (similar to identifier in the touch event).
pointerType	Integer that identifies whether the event came from a mouse, a stylus, or a finger.
pressure	The pen pressure from 0 to 255. According to Microsoft's documentation, this is available only with pen input.
rotation	Integer from 0 to 359. Rotation of the cursor, if supported.
tilt[X|Y]	The tilt of the stylus, only supported with pen input

The `pointerType` property is an enum and can be compared to contents on the `MSPointerEvent` object to identify it (**Listing 6.1**).

LISTING 6.1 Detecting pointer type

```
function handleEvent(event) {
    switch (event.pointerType) {

        case event.MSPOINTER_TYPE_TOUCH:
            //The pointer was a finger.
            break;
        case event.MSPOINTER_TYPE_PEN:
            // The pointer was a stylus
            break;
        case event.MSPOINTER_TYPE_MOUSE:
            // The pointer was a mouse
            break;
    }
}

element.addEventListener("MSPointerDown", handleEvent, false);
```

HANDLING TAPS

To demonstrate using tap events, we'll make a page with a button that toggles the visibility of a photograph (**Figure 6.1**).

FIGURE 6.1 A toggle button. © ibm4381/ Flickr. Made available under a Creative Commons Attribution 2.0 license.)

Rather than wait for the button click event, we'll listen for the `touchstart` event, which fires as soon as the user's finger touches the screen. Let's start with some simple HTML and CSS (**Listing 6.2**).

LISTING 6.2 Example markup

```
<!DOCTYPE html>
<html>
<head>
  <meta charset="utf-8">
  <meta http-equiv="X-UA-Compatible" content="IE=edge,chrome=1">
  <meta name="viewport" content="width=device-width">
  <title>Touch</title>
  <style type="text/css" media="screen">

    body {
      margin: 0;
      padding: 0;

      font-family: Helmet, Freesans, sans-serif;
      text-align: center;
    }

    .button {
      font-size: 16px;
      padding: 10px;
      font-weight: bold;
      border: 0;
      color: #fff;
      border-radius: 10px;
      box-shadow: inset 0px 1px 3px #fff, 0px 1px 2px #000;
      background: #ff3019;
      opacity: 1;
    }

    .active, .button:active {
      box-shadow: inset 0px 1px 3px #000, 0px 1px 2px #fff;
    }
```

```
    .picture {
        display: none;
    }
    </style>
</head>
<body>
    <div id="touchme">
        <button class="button" id="toggle">Toggle Picture</button>
        <div class="picture" style="display: none">
            <p>Goldfinch by ibm4381 on Flickr</p>
            <a href="http://www.flickr.com/photos/j_benson/3504443844/">
                <img src="img.jpg" width="320" height="256" alt="Goldfinch">
            </a>
        </div>
    </div>
</body>
</html>
```

Next we'll create a simple function to toggle the image:

```
function togglePicture(){
    var h = document.querySelector(".picture");
    if(h.style.display == "none") {
        h.style.display = "block";
    } else {
        h.style.display = "none";
    }
}
```

Then it's just a matter of attaching a listener to the touchstart event:

```
node.addEventListener('touchstart', function(e){
    e.preventDefault();
    togglePicture();
});
```

Try this example on a touch device and you'll notice the perceived performance improvement right away. To see the difference, change the touchstart event to a click event. There's one problem with this implementation: preventing the default behavior on the event caused the active state of the button to stop appearing. The active state is how the user knows that a tap was heard by the interface, so it's essential that this works.

Because we know when the touch starts and ends, we can simply swap classes when the active state should be active:

```
node.addEventListener('touchstart', function(e){
    e.preventDefault();
    e.target.className = "active button";
    togglePicture();
});

node.addEventListener('touchend', function(e){
    e.preventDefault();
    e.target.className = "button";
});
```

CREATING A SYNTHETIC TAP EVENT

The previous example will work only in browsers that support touch events, which means every mobile browser except IE10. It won't work on a desktop browser. I like to encapsulate components like that as much as possible, and if possible make them reusable. A convenient way to do this is to create a synthetic "tap" event. There are two ways to do this. One is to create a custom event infrastructure, like jQuery or YUI do. Another option is to use DOM Level 3 to actually create a custom event.

A custom event in the DOM behaves exactly like a normal DOM event. You can event subscribe with addEventListener. The difference is that you get to define when to fire the event, as well as the event's behavior. To create a tap event we'll use a custom event (**Listing 6.3**).

LISTING 6.3 Using custom DOM events

```
node.addEventListener('tap', function(e){
    togglePicture();
});

node.addEventListener('touchstart', function(e){
    //CustomEvent is a special event type
    var tap = document.createEvent('CustomEvent');
    tap.initCustomEvent('tap', true, true, null);
    node.dispatchEvent(tap);
});
```

The `initCustomEvent` method takes four parameters:

- The event name
- Whether or not the event bubbles
- Whether or not the event is cancelable
- Detail, which can be any arbitrary data passed when initializing the event

Doing it this this way doesn't give us much; we're still adding a touchstart listener, and clicks still don't work. A cleaner approach is a create a function to add the tap listener. Touch events are feature detected, and the event falls back to mouse events (**Listing 6.4**).

LISTING 6.4 Abstracting the custom event

```javascript
function addTapListener(node, callback) {

    //start by supporting mouseevents
    var startEvent = 'mousedown', endEvent = 'mouseup';

    //if touch events are available use them instead
    if (typeof(window.ontouchstart) != 'undefined') {
        //touch events work
        startEvent = 'touchstart';
        endEvent   = 'touchend';
    }

    node.addEventListener(startEvent, function(e) {
        var tap = document.createEvent('CustomEvent');
        tap.initCustomEvent('tap', true, true, null);
        node.dispatchEvent(tap);
    });

    node.addEventListener(endEvent, function(e) {
        var tapend = document.createEvent('CustomEvent');
        tapend.initCustomEvent('tapend', true, true, null);
        node.dispatchEvent(tapend);
    })

    node.addEventListener('tap', callback);
}
```

The tapend event is automatically created. Feature detection is as simple as checking for the existence of ontouchstart on the window object. With this function the toggle code looks like this:

```
addTapListener(document.getElementById('toggle'), function(e){
    e.preventDefault();
    e.target.className = 'active button';
    togglePicture();
});
```

```
node.addEventListener('tapend', function(e){
    e.preventDefault();
    e.target.className = "button";
});
```

There's no less code than in the first example, but it's much clearer what's happening and the code works on the desktop with no change.

A NODE FACADE

One of the things I love about libraries like YUI and jQuery is how they've created facades around DOM nodes to simplify event handling. So rather than use the slightly ugly function we created earlier, we can create a chainable facade for a node that has an on function. The on function will let us listen to any DOM event, or synthetic events we might define. In this case we'll just create a tap and tapend even. With the new mini-library, we can do this (notice the chained functions):

```
$('.button').on('tap', function(e) {
    e.preventDefault();
    togglePicture();
    e.target.className = "active button";
}).on('tapend', function(e) {
    e.target.className = "button";
});
```

In this example, $ is a function that returns an object. The object has just one method (for now) called on. The on method returns the same object to support chaining. Let's start with the feature detection code, to figure out what events to listen to (**Listing 6.5**).

LISTING 6.5 Using a node facade

```
(function(){

  var TOUCHSTART, TOUCHEND;

  //normal touch events
  if (typeof(window.ontouchstart) != 'undefined') {

    TOUCHSTART = 'touchstart';
    TOUCHEND   = 'touchend';

  //microsoft touch events
  } else if (typeof(window.onmspointerdown) != 'undefined') {
    TOUCHSTART = 'MSPointerDown';
    TOUCHEND   = 'MSPointerUp';
  } else {
    TOUCHSTART = 'mousedown';
    TOUCHEND   = 'mouseup';
  }
```

This code runs only once, when the script is first parsed and executed, there's no sense in rerunning these checks, because the browser won't change after the script is loaded. Next we'll define a constructor for the node facade that will keep a reference to the actual DOM node:

```
function NodeFacade(node){

  this._node = node;

}

NodeFacade.prototype.getDomNode = function() {
  return this._node;
}
```

In case the facade isn't enough, there's a getter for the underlying DOM node.

Next come the on and off functions. This is what will actually attach and remove the event handlers.

```
NodeFacade.prototype.on = function(evt, callback) {

    if (evt === 'tap') {
        this._node.addEventListener(TOUCHSTART, callback);
    } else if (evt === 'tapend') {
        this._node.addEventListener(TOUCHEND, callback);
    } else {
        this._node.addEventListener(evt, callback);
    }

    return this;

}


NodeFacade.prototype.off = function(evt, callback) {
    if (evt === 'tap') {
        this._node.removeEventListener(TOUCHSTART, callback);
    } else if (evt === 'tapend') {
        this._node.removeEventListener(TOUCHEND, callback);
    } else {
        this._node.removeEventListener(evt, callback);
    }

    return this;
}
```

Because 'tap' and 'tapend' aren't real events, we can bind them instead to whatever was defined for the TOUCHSTART and TOUCHEND constants. All other DOM events are simply passed through.

The "$" function just needs to find the node based on the selector and instantiate a new node facade:

```
window.$ = function(selector) {
    var node = document.querySelector(selector);

    if(node) {
        return new NodeFacade(node);
    } else {
        return null;
    }
}
```

```
})();
```

Now the actual logic that drives the picture-toggling page is as simple and clear as can be:

```
$('.button').on('tap', function(e) {
    e.preventDefault();
    togglePicture();
    e.target.className = "active button";
}).on('tapend', function(e) {
    e.target.className = "button";
});
```

WRAPPING UP

In this chapter you learned the basics of touch events, along with a nice trick to improve perceived performance by using taps instead of clicks. You also learned a couple of patterns for creating synthetic events, including creating a node facade.

When working with touch events, keep in mind the browser (and device) native events, like "double tap to zoom." Remember that preventing default on a touch event can override native events, so be sure to test your interactions to make sure you haven't broken a user expectation.

PROJECT

Looking back at the Bird Quiz, rebuild the event system to use taps rather than clicks.

- This should work on iOS, Android, and IE10.
- Make sure the Submit and radio buttons give immediate feedback when the user taps.
- Clicks should work seamlessly on a desktop browser.

CHAPTER 7

CSS Transitions, Animation, and Transforms

When you do things right, people won't be sure you've done anything at all.

—Futurama

Every Internet user has experienced the evil: intro animations, dancing, and blinking text. Everyone has also experienced the good, but ideally users don't even remember the good. When used correctly, animation serves a purpose in the UI. It explains the result of a user's interaction. Almost every change on the screen in iOS is accompanied by an animation explaining what happened.

In the toggle example from the previous chapter, the image "pops" in. It's a little jarring and it's not clear what happened to the image. Instead the image could slide off to the right or left, indicating to the user that the image is still there and could be brought back.

Performance problems become glaring when things move on the screen. Call it "jitter," "jank," or "hiccups," animation that doesn't perform makes an application feel slow. On touch devices, animation is central to giving users feedback for the gestures. If those animations are slow, the gesture itself feels slow.

ANIMATING ELEMENTS

Traditionally, elements are animated using setTimeout (**Listing 7.1**). Calling the same function recursively changes values over time.

LISTING 7.1 Animation with SetTimeout

```
function fadeIn() {
   var h = document.querySelector(".picture");
   var opacity = parseFloat(h.style.opacity);
   if(opacity < 1) {
      opacity = opacity + 0.1;
      h.style.opacity = opacity;
      window.setTimeout(fadeIn, 33);
   }
}
```

This approach can result in jittery animation. All JavaScript in a browser executes in a single thread: only one piece of code can be executed at a time. Asynchronous tasks like event timers are queued and then executed when the thread becomes idle. In the example above, if the browser is busy, the next frame won't be drawn until it's not busy, causing a noticeable jitter in the animation. Additionally, while the code inside the timer is being executed, nothing else can happen. That means event handlers are queued.

If the code inside the timer is too slow it can seriously degrade the responsiveness of the interface, especially on slow mobile devices. This can be overcome somewhat by increasing the delay between timeouts, but increasing the delay makes the animation start to look jittery anyway.

For these reasons I suggest you try to avoid setTimeout animation. For most tasks, CSS transitions can achieve the effect you want and the experience will be much better.

TRANSITIONS

CSS transitions are the simplest animations to do in CSS. The power of transitions is that they execute in a *separate thread* from the JavaScript. On mobile devices with multiple cores, smooth animation is possible while JavaScript execution thread is working. Animation puts a strain on the CPU, of course, but it won't degrade the script's ability to handle events in a timely manner. Effectively CSS animation and transitions let you have your cake and eat it too: you can have a more dynamic interface with animation and still keep event handlers moving quickly.

The concept is simple: any *animatable* CSS property can be animated with a transition.

NOTE: Most properties that take a value are animatable; a complete list can be found at the W3C website (http://www.w3.org/TR/css3-transitions/#animatable-properties).

A change in the animated CSS value triggers the animation. Transitions are applied using the CSS `transition` property. The syntax is as follows:

```
transition: [property] [duration] [timing-function] [delay];
```

The property can be a list of properties; all of the values are optional. For example, `this:transition: color 1s ease-out` specifies a one-second color that slows down toward the end of the transition. Although transitions are now standardized, WebKit still requires a prefix; IE 10, Opera, and Firefox Mobile have dropped the prefix.

> **NOTE:** The `all` keyword can be used to animate any animatable property that changes. I don't recommend using this because it can lead to unintended animation and impact performance.

In Appendix C (which you can download at touch-interfaces.com), "Building a Mobile Web Application," we use an example that hides and shows an image on taps. The experience would be better if the image faded in and out quickly, rather than just popping in and out. To do this we need to make a couple changes in the HTML to simplify the styles. **Listing 7.2** shows the HTML that gives the hidden element a picture class as the base class. Then the hidden class becomes a generic class that applies the change.

LISTING 7.2 Creating a hidden image

```
<div id="touchme">
   <button class="button" id="toggle">Toggle Picture</button>
   <div class="picture hidden">
      <p>Goldfinch by ibm4381 on Flickr</p>
      <a href="http://www.flickr.com/photos/j_benson/3504443844/">
         <img src="img.jpg" width="320" height="256" alt="Goldfinch">
      </a>
   </div>
</div>
```

Listing 7.3 shows the transitions applied using CSS.

LISTING 7.3 Applying transitions via CSS

```
.picture {
   -webkit-transition: opacity 0.2s ease-out;
   transition: opacity 0.2s ease-out;
   opacity: 1;
}

.picture.hidden {
   opacity: 0;
}
```

Listing 7.4 shows the script adapted a little to swap styles rather than change property values.

LISTING 7.4 Swapping styles

```
var hidden = true;
var h = document.querySelector(".picture");

function togglePicture(){
   if(hidden) {
      h.className = "picture";
      hidden = false;
   } else {
      h.className = "picture hidden";
      hidden = true;
   }
}

$('.button').on('tap', function(e) {
   e.preventDefault();
   togglePicture();
   e.target.className = "active button";
}).on('tapend', function(e) {
   e.target.className = "button";
});
```

Now when the user taps on the toggle button the picture will gracefully fade in and out.

USING TRANSITIONS WITH JAVASCRIPT

As shown above, transitions make it very simple to add smooth animation. In addition to the CSS functions, transitions fire a `transitionend` event when they finish. This event makes it possible to use transitions for more complex animations. For example, we can make a page with a cool bouncing ball (**Figure 7.1**).

A bouncing ball accelerates downward, stops, and then decelerates on the way up. So first we need to apply a transition, change the value, and fire off the transition. Then, when the transition is done we'll apply a different transition to send the ball back to the top. As shown in **Listing 7.5**, the HTML is very simple:

LISTING 7.5 Bouncing ball markup

```
<div id="ball">

</div>
<div id="floor">

</div>
```

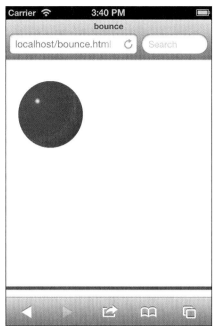

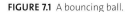
FIGURE 7.1 A bouncing ball.

The style sheet just sets up the look; the transitions all live in JavaScript. **Listing 7.6** omits the gradients that give the ball its 3D look for space. The code on the website contains the full styles.

LISTING 7.6 Bouncing ball styles

```
body {
    margin: 0;
    padding: 0;
}

/* Turn a square into a circle */
#ball {
    background: red;
    height: 100px;
    width: 100px;
    position: absolute;
    top: 10px;
    left: 20px;
    border-radius: 50px;
}
```

```
#floor {
    position: absolute;
    bottom: 10px;
    left: 0px;
    width: 350px;
    height: 1px;
    border-top: 5px solid brown;
}
```

The full JavaScript for the next part can be found in **Listing 7.7** on the website, but we'll step through it here. First we need to do some feature detection to deal with the fact that some browsers prefix transitions and the `transitionend` event.

LISTING 7.7 Detecting the correct vendor prefixes

```
(function(){

    var down = false,
        trans = 'transition';
        eventName = 'transitionend';

    //use prefix if necessary
    if(typeof document.body.style.webkitTransition === 'string') {
        trans = 'webkitTransition';
        eventName = 'webkitTransitionEnd';
    } else if (typeof document.body.style.MozTransition === 'string') {
        trans = 'MozTransition';
    }
```

To get this effect with transitions we'll use a timing function. Ease-in and ease-out, while simple, aren't quite right for this effect. What we need is a custom easing function. In addition to the easing keywords (ease-in, ease-out, ease-in-out) there's another option, `cubic-bezier`. The syntax seems a little opaque, but it's actually pretty simple. The function defines a curve with four points (**Figure 7.2**).

The four values describe the positions of the control points (P1 and P2). The other two points are always at 0,0 and 1,1. If you've ever used a vector drawing program like Illustrator you know what the control points do: they control the curve of the graph. The graph above is the same as ease-in-out, equivalent to `cubic-bezier(0.42, 0, 0.58, 1.0)`.

For the bouncing ball animation we'll create a curve more like **Figure 7.3** on the way down, and like **Figure 7.4** on the way up.

These curves will give the ball constant acceleration on the way up and on the way down. `Cubic-bezier(0, .27, .32, 1)` will work well on the way up, and `cubic-bezier(1, 0, 0.96, 0.91)` will work on the way down.

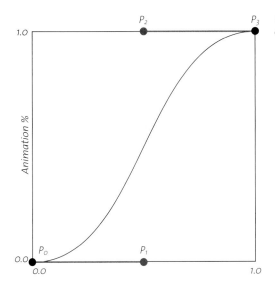

FIGURE 7.2 Cubic Bézier curve for ease-in and ease-out.

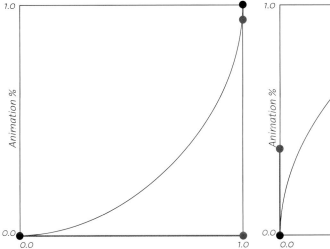

FIGURE 7.3 Cubic Bézier curve for a falling ball.

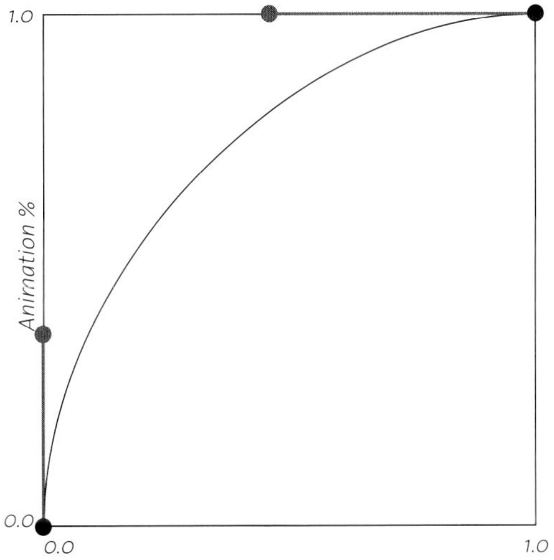

FIGURE 7.4 Cubic Bézier curve for a bouncing ball.

NOTE: There are several tools that let you play with Bézier curves in the browser to get the right feel. Just search for "CSS cubic-bezier tool."

Now that we know the curves we want to apply, we can write a bounce function:

```
var ball = document.getElementById('ball'),
    floor = document.getElementById('floor');

function bounce() {
    if(down) {
        //trans is the prefixed css property
        ball.style[trans] = "top 1s cubic-bezier(0, .27, .32, 1)";
        ball.style.top = '10px';
        down = false;
    } else {
        ball.style[trans] = "top 1s cubic-bezier(1, 0, 0.96, 0.91)";
        ball.style.top = (floor.offsetTop - 100) + 'px';
        down = true;
    }
}

//eventName was defined above as the correct event
//name for this browser (webkitTransitionEnd/transitionend)
ball.addEventListener(eventName, bounce);
bounce();

})();
```

Now the ball bounces forever.

CSS ANIMATION

CSS transitions, despite the bouncing ball example, are still primarily useful as actual transitions between states. At a certain point you need something more powerful. CSS animations are the answer. Rather than defining an animation between two states, CSS animations let you define multiple keyframes in animations. Each keyframe represents a state in the animation and the browser smoothly transitions between them.

CSS animations are also very likely to cause you repetitive motion injuries because WebKit (and slightly older versions of Firefox and Opera) still require vendor prefixes for animation, so each animation, keyframe, and property must be defined separately for each prefix.

With animations we can recreate the bouncing ball, this time using only CSS.

CREATING KEYFRAMES

Keyframes are created with the @keyframes rule. Inside is a list of "times," CSS blocks representing the keyframes in the animation. The times are defined relatively as a percentage of the animation. For the animation to work at all there must be at least a 0 percent and 100 percent time defined. To create a basic bounce, the keyframes look like **Listing 7.8**.

LISTING 7.8 Defining @keyframes

```
@keyframes bounce {
    0% {
        top: 20px;
    }

    50% {
        top: 300px;
    }

    100% {
        top: 20px;
    }
}
```

At the beginning of the animation, the ball is at the top; in the middle, it's on the ground; and at the end, it's back at the top. Once keyframes are defined they can be applied to any selector with the animation property:

```
#ball {
    animation: bounce 2s infinite;
}
```

The name of the keyframes comes first, followed by the duration and the iteration count. In this case we want the bounce to last forever so we'll use the "infinite" keyword. The animation property is shorthand for a full set of animation properties. The same animation can be defined with sub-properties. This is shown a little more clearly, but with a few more bytes, in **Listing 7.9**.

LISTING 7.9 Using animation sub-properties

```
#ball {
    animation-name: bounce;
    animation duration: 2s;
    animation-iteration-count: infinite;
}
```

This animation is still missing one thing: the timing functions we used before to make the jump more realistic. As with transitions, a timing function can be applied to the animation. For keyframes, the timing function can be applied to the animation in the selector, or different timing functions can be applied to each time in the @keyframes rule. If a timing function is defined in the selector, a timing function in a keyframe will override that function.

Of course, thanks to vendor prefixes, this CSS won't work in all browsers. Instead the @keyframes rule needs to be repeated for each vendor prefix (comma syntax is not allowed), and the animation properties also need to be repeated for each vendor. The complete, prefixed version of the animation with timing function follows. If you're faint of heart, don't look at the styles shown in **Listing 7.10**, you may find the excessive use of prefixes disturbing.

LISTING 7.10 Creating CSS animation with cubic Bézier timing functions and vendor prefixes

```
/* WebKit */
@-webkit-keyframes bounce {
   0% {
      top: 20px;
      -webkit-animation-timing-function: cubic-bezier(1, 0, 0.96, 0.91);
   }

   50% {
      top: 300px;
      -webkit-animation-timing-function: cubic-bezier(0, 0.27, 0.32, 1);
   }

   100% {
      top: 20px;
      -webkit-animation-timing-function: cubic-bezier(0, 0.27, 0.32, 1);
   }
}

/* Firefox < 16*/
@-moz-keyframes bounce {
   0% {
      top: 20px;
      -moz-animation-timing-function: cubic-bezier(1, 0, 0.96, 0.91);
   }

   50% {
      top: 300px;
```

```
        -moz-animation-timing-function: cubic-bezier(0, 0.27, 0.32, 1);
    }


    100% {
        top: 20px;
        -moz-animation-timing-function: cubic-bezier(0, 0.27, 0.32, 1);
    }
}


/* Opera < 12.1*/
@-o-keyframes bounce {
    0% {
        top: 20px;
        -o-animation-timing-function: cubic-bezier(1, 0, 0.96, 0.91);
    }


    50% {
        top: 300px;
        -o-animation-timing-function: cubic-bezier(0, 0.27, 0.32, 1);
    }


    100% {
        top: 20px;
        -o-animation-timing-function: cubic-bezier(0, 0.27, 0.32, 1);
    }
}


/* W3C / IE10 / Firefox / opera */
@keyframes bounce {
    0% {
        top: 20px;
        animation-timing-function: cubic-bezier(1, 0, 0.96, 0.91);
    }


    50% {
        top: 300px;
        animation-timing-function: cubic-bezier(0, 0.27, 0.32, 1);
    }
```

```
    100% {
      top: 20px;
      animation-timing-function: cubic-bezier(0, 0.27, 0.32, 1);
    }
}

#floor {
  top: 400px;
}

#ball {
  -webkit-animation: 2s bounce infinite;
  -moz-animation: 2s bounce infinite;
  -ms-animation: 2s bounce infinite;
  -o-animation: 2s bounce infinite;
  animation-duration: 2s;
  animation-name: bounce;
  animation-iteration-count: infinite;
  animation-timing-function: linear;
}
```

As you can see, the prefix situation is pretty bad at the moment. The W3C syntax is high-lighted; hopefully WebKit will drop prefixes soon and this will get much less painful to use.

After applying this wordy CSS essentially the same animation will now appear, but this time without any JavaScript at all for animation. If we want even more control over animations we could add event listeners for the animation events: animationstart, animationend, and animationiteration. The events are not as close to standardization. For reference, **Table 8.1** shows the events in the major mobile browsers.

TABLE 8.1 Animation events

W3C/FIREFOX	WEBKIT	OPERA	IE10
animationstart	webkitAnimationStart	oanimationstart	animationstart
animation	webkitAnimationIteration	oanimationiteration	animationiteration
animationstart	webkitAnimationEnd	oanimationend	animationend

NOTE: For complete documentation of CSS animations, see https://developer.mozilla.org/en-US/docs/CSS/animation.

JAVASCRIPT ANIMATION REVISITED

CSS animations and transitions are preferable to JavaScript animation, but inevitably you'll come across a situation where CSS animation won't work and you still need to build animations with JavaScript. In this case you don't need to turn back to `setTimeout`.

The goal for animations is generally to have them appear as smooth as possible. There should be no jitter, no weird pauses. Although smoothness is subjective, you can say certain things objectively about a smooth animation. A smooth animation has a higher frame rate. The frame rate is a measurement of how many times per second the element is redrawn. A movie has a frame rate of 24 frames per second (FPS). Most video games target 60.

A smooth animation also portrays motion correctly: an animation shouldn't suddenly stop or skip ahead. CSS animation is designed for animation so the underlying code works to optimize for smoothness. Rather than freeze or hiccup, the frame rate of a CSS animation is automatically lowered.

Another reason `setTimeout` doesn't perform well is that rather than optimizing for motion, `setTimeout` optimizes for the interval. The code tries to get the timeout to execute at the right time. If you've built an animation around 33-millisecond timeouts you might think you'd get in 30 FPS, but if the script is busy the timeout is queued for execution, or in the case of `setInterval` it's dropped. Both behaviors result in making things looks more jittery than they should. So what can you do?

REQUESTANIMATIONFRAME

Modern browsers have given us a new and more powerful tool for JavaScript animation. Rather than `setTimeout` there's a better-suited DOM method: `requestAnimationFrame`. Rather than a time and a callback, `requestAnimationFrame` takes only a callback. Rather than firing the callback after a time, the callback is fired before the next time the browser is repainted. This allows the browser itself to optimize things, including the frame rate, to improve performance. Also, by combining UI updates, the CPU load is much lower than `setTimeout`.

That's the good news. The bad news is that `requestAnimationFrame` is prefixed, and it doesn't work in the Android browser at all (it does work on Chrome for Android). The small piece of code in **Listing 7.11** creates a wrapper function to hide browser normalization. In addition to adding prefixes we'll add a `setTimeout` fallback. To limit the performance problems of `setTimeout` we'll limit the frame rate to 15 FPS, not great, but also less likely to cause queuing and other performance problems.

LISTING 7.11 Creating a browser neutral request frame function

```
//a function to build a function, so browser checks only run once
var requestFrame = (function() {
  var thisFunc,
    prefixList = ['webkit', 'moz', 'ms'];

  //check each method for availability, when one is found,
  //use that
```

```
        for (var i=0; i < prefixList.length; i++) {
          thisFunc = prefixList[i] + 'RequestAnimationFrame';

          if(window[thisFunc]) {
            return function(callback) {
              window[thisFunc](callback);
            }
          }
        }

        //if we got here none was found, fallback to 15 FPS setTimeout
        return function(callback) {
          window.setTimeout(callback, 67);
        }

    })();
```

Basic animation is simple: to move the ball from the earlier example down 500 pixels, 10 pixels per frame:

```
(function(){

    var destination = 500;
    var start = 0;

    var ball = document.getElementById('ball');

    function move(element){
      start = start + 10;
      element.style.top = (start) + 'px';

      if (start < destination) {
        requestFrame(function(){
          move(element);
        });
      }
    }

    move(ball);

})();
```

Because the frame rate is dynamic and controlled by the browser, this animation may move slower or faster depending on the device. To make sure the animation moves at a constant speed we need to figure out how much time has elapsed between frames and then decide how much the element should move based on the total time we want the animation to last (**Listing 7.12**).

LISTING 7.12 Animating with requestAnimationFrame

```javascript
function animate(element, from, to, duration, callback) {

  //figure out how much to move per millisecond
  var pixelsPerMS = Math.abs(from-to)/duration;

  //keep track of the position
  var pos = from;

  //keep track of the time
  var time = Date.now();

  //create the callback function
  var func = function(){

    var lastTime, elapsed, pixelsToMove;

    lastTime = time;
    time = Date.now();
    elapsed = time - lastTime;

    //multiply the time elapsed by how many pixels
    //per ms to determine how far to move
    pixelsToMove = Math.ceil(elapsed * pixelsPerMS);

    pos = pos + pixelsToMove;

    //In real life this should do more than move elements
    //down.
    element.style.top = pos + 'px';

    if( pos < to ){
      requestFrame(func);
    } else {
```

```
        callback();
      }

    }

  func();

}

//move the ball 100 pixels in 5 seconds
animate(ball, 0, 100, 5000, function(){
  console.log('done!');
});
```

This supports a callback function, so callers can be notified when the animation is finished.

MAKING ANIMATION BUTTERY SMOOTH

So far we've covered some tools that help make animations perform better. Just using these tools won't be enough to make your animations beautifully smooth. Mobile users have been trained to expect buttery smooth animations from native apps.

DEBUGGING ANIMATION PERFORMANCE PROBLEMS

Slow animation is hard to miss but it can be quite difficult to identify why an animation is slow. Chrome has an incredibly powerful tool in the Chrome Developer Tools: the frames timeline. The frames timeline lets you see what the frame rate is, and more importantly identify what's affecting it. This tool is available only in Chrome for the desktop, but it's a very good proxy for what might be causing performance issues on WebKit mobile browsers and less reliably on non-WebKit browsers like IE 10 or Firefox Mobile.

The timeline looks like **Figure 7.5**.

The tools mentioned in this chapter certainly make animation smoother. But they don't solve the fundamental problem with animation: you're asking the browser to do something over and over again. If that thing is a little slow, animation multiplies the performance problem. Generally speaking, 30 FPS looks OK, 60 FPS is buttery smooth. At 60 FPS a frame lasts 16 and 2/3 milliseconds.

The graph on the top represents frames. The bars represent the time spent on each frame. As the bars get bigger, meaning the time to execute a frame was longer, the overall frame rate declines. In the screenshot each frame is short enough that the frame rate is consistently better than 60 FPS. You can see that there are lines representing both 30 and 60 FPS.

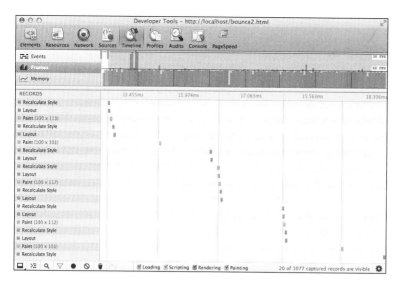

FIGURE 7.5
The Chrome Developer Tools frames timeline.

If you make a change in the DOM that takes 30 ms but do it only once, the user probably won't notice. But if you try to animate that operation the frame rate will be effectively capped at around 30 FPS. This same rule applies to "native" animations as well, such as scrolling. If your page is too slow to draw in 16.667 ms, the frame rate of scrolling will slow down, making your page *feel* slower. So the trick to smooth animation is a higher frame rate. And you get a higher frame rate by spending less time making the DOM changes you want on each frame.

The big problem with this tool being available only on desktop is that, compared to mobile devices, desktops are supercomputers. When we add a large image to the background of the page, then add a drop shadow to the ball, the animation really slows down on an Android device. On the desktop the animation runs fine. To really dig in to the performance issues we need to use the bottom pane, which shows what the browser is doing during each frame. By clicking on one of the bars we can zoom into the waterfall graph for just that frame (**Figure 7.6**).

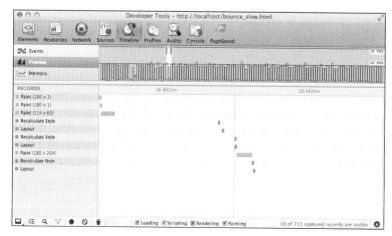

FIGURE 7.6
The frames waterfall graph.

The frame duration is pretty good. Looking at the detail, however, we can see the effect of my DOM writes (recalculate style and layout), which aren't too bad. The big green bar is probably the culprit for the slowness on the Galaxy. That green bar represents the repaint time. The repaint is when the browser actually renders an image to the area of the browser window that changed. This is more work if the area is bigger, so more animation or animations that cover a larger space are slower. Its speed also depends on how complex the rendering task was. If the browser just had to redraw a small black rectangle, that's pretty easy. When you have a large round ball with a drop shadow, that's quite a bit harder. The reason is compositing.

COMPOSITING

Compositing is when the browser has to draw an image over another one. A computer screen is a flat layer of pixels, so to render an image the browser and ultimately the graphics toolkit in the OS has to calculate what color to make each pixel. Drawing a black rectangle is easy because the calculation is easy. If the pixel is in the rectangle, it's black; if it isn't, the pixel is white. For an anti-aliased circle like the ball in the animation, the calculation is harder because the edge pixels are partially transparent. Whatever system is doing the rendering has to compute the color of the edge pixels based on the rules that allow smooth edges. When you add a drop shadow or make an element partially transparent the problem gets harder because there are many more pixels to compute. If something transparent has to pass over something with a drop shadow, the problem is compounded. As the element grows, the number of pixels that need to be drawn grows exponentially, again making the calculation more difficult.

Compositing is expensive. So when you animate an element, the less compositing the browser needs to do the faster it will be. If the drawing task is difficult, you'll see in the Chrome waterfall graph that "paint" tasks get longer and longer. If an animation is purely CSS, but still slow, compositing is often the culprit.

CSS TRANSFORMS

After you've optimized all your animations you might find that they're still not fast enough. It's time to bring in the big guns: CSS transforms. CSS transforms let you change the way an element is drawn after the DOM calculations are made. A CSS transform is applied with the transform CSS property, followed by one or more transform functions (**Table 7.2**).

For example, to move an element relative to its normal position in the DOM, you can use the translate transform function. Translate takes two parameters, representing how much to translate the element from its origin. By default the origin is the center of the element.

TABLE 7.2 Core CSS transform functions

SYNTAX	DESCRIPTION
translate(x,y)	Move element horizontally (x) and vertically (y) units from the origin. Values must be specified in CSS units.
translate[X|Y](amount)	Move the element horizontally or vertically.
scale(multiple, [y multiple])	Scale the element.
scale[XY](multiple)	Scale the element horizontally or vertically.
rotate(deg)	Rotate the element (degrees or radians).
skew[X|Y](deg)	Skew the element horizontally or vertically (degrees or radians).
matrix([matrix])	Apply a two-dimensional transformation matrix.
translate3d(x,y,z)	Translate the element in three dimensions.
scale3d(x,y,z)	Scale the element in three dimensions.
rotate3d(x,y,x, deg)	Rotate the element around the specified axis.
matrix3d([matrix)	Apply a 3D transformation matrix.

This CSS causes the #ball element to move as it's tapped (**Listing 7.13**).

LISTING 7.13 Replacing positioning with CSS transforms

```
#ball {
    top: 10px;
    left: 10px;
}

#ball:active {
    top: 50px;
    left: 0px;
}
```

The same effect can be achieved with transforms:

```
#ball {
    top: 10px;
    left: 10px;
}

#ball:active {
    top: 10px;
    left: 10px;
```

```
    /* only webkit requires a prefix,
    -webkit-transform: translate(0, 40px);
    transform: translate(0, 40px);
}
```

If I go back and modify the bouncing ball animation to use transforms rather than translate like so:

```
@keyframes bounce {
    0% {
        transform: translate(0, 20px);
        animation-timing-function: cubic-bezier(1, 0, 0.96, 0.91);
    }

    50% {
        transform: translate(0, 300px);
        animation-timing-function: cubic-bezier(0, 0.27, 0.32, 1);
    }

    100% {
        transform: translate(0, 20px);
        animation-timing-function: cubic-bezier(0, 0.27, 0.32, 1);
    }
}
```

The frames graph changes from what's shown in **Figure 7.7** to what's shown in **Figure 7.8**.

FIGURE 7.7 The frames graph with normal CSS positioning.

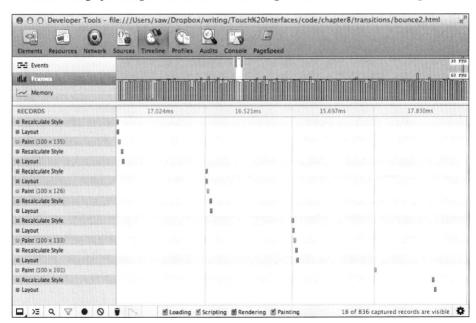

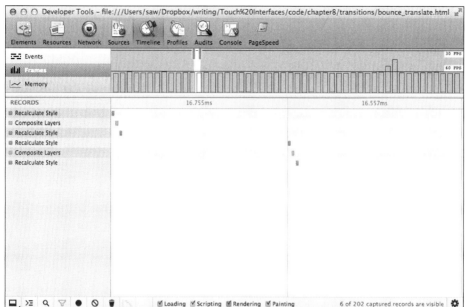

FIGURE 7.8
The frames graph using transforms.

On a desktop the frame rate does not change, but you can clearly see that the browser is doing less work with transforms. When tested on a Galaxy, the performance is noticeably improved.

> **NOTE:** For detailed documentation of all the features of CSS transforms, visit developer.mozilla.org/en-US/docs/CSS/Using_CSS_transforms.

HARDWARE ACCELERATION

When I first saw the iPhone in action I was struck by how smooth the animation was, particularly with gradients, drop shadows, and other expensive graphic effects. Apple achieved that performance because the device—like every iOS device since—shipped with built-in graphics acceleration hardware. GPUs are designed for animation and compositing. On devices that have GPUs, browsers try to use the GPU for acceleration where they can. Transforms might be rendered on the GPU, but 3D transforms are always rendered there. Hardware-accelerated transforms are by far the fastest animations. To convert the 2D transforms we just used we just need to change `translate` to `translate3d` and add a Z value. Even though the Z value is zero and there's no actual transformation in the third dimension, this transform will be offloaded to the graphics hardware (**Listing 7.14**).

LISTING 7.14 Accelerating hardware with translate3d

```
@keyframes bounce {
    0% {
        transform: translate3d(0, 20px, 0);
        animation-timing-function: cubic-bezier(1, 0, 0.96, 0.91);
    }

    50% {
        transform: translate3d(0, 300px, 0);
        animation-timing-function: cubic-bezier(0, 0.27, 0.32, 1);
    }

    100% {
        transform: translate3d(0, 20px, 0);
        animation-timing-function: cubic-bezier(0, 0.27, 0.32, 1);
    }
}
```

On a Galaxy, the animation is now quite smooth, probably between 30 and 60 FPS. It seems a bit like magic. In many cases, hardware acceleration is the solution to making smooth animation.

THE LIMITS OF HARDWARE ACCELERATION

When the browser decides that an element should be hardware accelerated it can't hand the native DOM element to the GPU. Instead it renders the element into an image and sends that image to the GPU. The GPU applies the image as a texture map to a polygon representing the element. Then the GPU can very quickly move the polygon around. If the bitmap had transparency information (an alpha channel), the element can be partially transparent. The GPU can scale the element up and down, rotate it, or apply transforms natively. What it can't do is rerender the contents. Once an element has been sent to the GPU, it's merely an image of the contents, not the actual contents.

Listing 7.15 shows the difference with a desktop browser.

LISTING 7.15 Comparing 2D transforms to 3D transforms

```
<head>
    <meta name="viewport" content="width=device-width">
    <style type="text/css">
    h1 {
        width: 100px;
        border: 1px solid black;
        margin: 50px 0px 100px 100px;
```

```
      text-align: center;
      font-size: 32px;
      -webkit-transform: scale(3);
transform: scale(3);
   }

   .blurry {
      -webkit-transform: scale3d(3,3,0);
      transform: scale3d(3,3,0);
   }

   </style>
</head>
<body>
   <h1>Hello</h1>
   <h1 class="blurry">Hello</h1>
</div>
</body>
```

Fully rendered, the top element with 2D transforms is sharp, and the bottom element with 3D transforms is blurry (**Figure 7.9**).

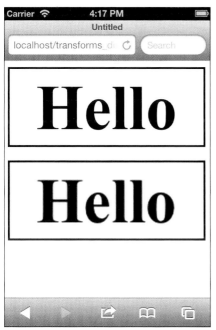

FIGURE 7.9 3D transforms can modify only the rendered image, resulting in a blurred image when scaled up.

The 3D transform resulted in blurry text. Because the 2D transform didn't require an image to be rendered, the browser was able to rerender the text at a larger size. The GPU had nothing but the image to work from, so it could only scale up the image, resulting in the blurry, interpolated version. To work around this limitation we can "scrub" transforms from elements once an animation is complete. Unless I'm truly doing something 3D (which is rare), I can convert a 3D transform back to a 2D transform when the animation is complete by changing the style when the `transitionend` or `animationend` events fire. In **Listing 7.16**, the element scales up when tapped, becoming blurred. After a moment the element will sharpen back up.

LISTING 7.16 Scrubbing transforms

```
<head>
    <meta charset="utf-8">
    <meta http-equiv="X-UA-Compatible" content="IE=edge,chrome=1">
    <meta name="viewport" content="width=device-width">
    <title>Touch</title>
    <style type="text/css">
        #zoomer {
            font-size: 24px;
            position: absolute;
            top:50px;
            left:100px;
            background: green;
            -webkit-transition: -webkit-transform .2s ease-in-out;
            transition: transform .2s ease-in-out;
        }
    </style>
</head>
<body>
    <h1 id="zoomer">Drink me!</h1>
</body>
<script type="text/javascript" charset="utf-8">
(function(){

    var TRANSFORM_PROPERTY =
        (typeof document.body.style.webkitTransform ==='string') ?
        'webkitTransform' : 'transform';
```

```
var TRANSFORM_END =
  (typeof document.body.style.webkitTransform ==='string') ?
  'webkitTransformEnd' : 'transformend';



function embiggen(element) {
  element.addEventListener(TRANSFORM_END, function(e) {
    element.style[TRANSFORM_PROPERTY] = 'scale(2)';
  });
  element.style[TRANSFORM_PROPERTY] = 'scale3d(2,2,0)';
}

var z = document.getElementById('zoomer');

z.addEventListener('click', function(e) {
  embiggen(z);
});

})();
</script>
```

We only had to check if the WebKit prefix was needed because none of the other widely installed mobile browsers require it. Scrubbing transforms this way has another benefit: freeing up graphics memory. Theoretically devices use shared memory: the GPU uses the same memory as the device, so there's as much memory available to the GPU as to the device. If you were developing a native game this would be the case. In the browser the picture is much more complex. The browser is doing a lot of work to make sure it uses the available device memory properly, including swapping memory to slower flash storage when necessary.

An element with a 3D transform reserves at least the space required to store the image representing the element in live memory controlled by the GPU. Although the software that runs the GPU (openGL on iPhone and Android) will attempt to manage resources as efficiently as possible, memory will still fill up (the GPU cannot swap memory to the flash storage). When the GPU is out of space, the browser will either act very strangely or it will crash. This is why you can't just apply `translate3d` to every element on the page to speed things up. Ideally you'll only use 3D transforms when you need them, and make sure to clean up when you're done.

If you apply multiple transforms, maintain the state of the element outside the DOM, so you don't need to read from the DOM again.

ENTER THE MATRIX

There are two transform functions that are a little different from the others. Rather than describe the operation you're trying to accomplish, they just take a series of numbers. These functions give you direct access to the underlying math in all the CSS transforms. This can be very powerful for more advanced operations in JavaScript, but it can also greatly simplify the task of maintaining the state of elements in JavaScript, without resorting to inspecting the DOM. Another benefit is that when you actually do inspect the DOM the `getComputed-Style()` value for the transform is always expressed as a matrix transform.

UNDERSTANDING TRANSFORMATION MATRICES

A matrix is grid of numbers, just like a mini-spreadsheet. 2D transforms are always 3x3 matrices. For 2D matrices, the first four values specify the matrix and the last two specify the translation (**Figure 7.10**).

FIGURE 7.10
Using the 2D matrix.

$$\begin{bmatrix} 1 & 2 & 5 \\ 3 & 4 & 6 \\ 0 & 0 & 1 \end{bmatrix}$$

The matrix above would be specified in CSS like this:

```
transform: matrix(1, 2, 3, 4, 5, 6);
```

2D transform syntax takes only six values, because the bottom row of the matrix always contains the values 0,0,1, so there's no need to specify them.

To apply the matrix, it's multiplied by the matrix representing the coordinates of each corner of the element's bounding box. This sounds confusing, but for the purposes of translation, you don't need to understand the matrix at all. You just need to know two things: the identity matrix and that only two (or three for 3D transforms) values actually affect translation at all. The identity matrix (**Figure 7.11**) is a transform that has no effect.

FIGURE 7.11
The identity matrix.

$$\begin{bmatrix} 1 & 0 & 0 \\ 0 & 1 & 0 \\ 0 & 0 & 1 \end{bmatrix}$$

The identity matrix is specified in CSS like so:

```
-webkit-transform: matrix(1,0,0,1,0,0);
transform: matrix(1,0,0,1,0,0);
```

To translate the object, just change the last two values, highlighted in Figure 7.11. You don't need units; pixels are assumed. So to move the element 10 pixels right and 20 pixels down, the matrix would look like this:

```
-webkit-transform: matrix(1,0,0,1,10,20);
transform: matrix(1,0,0,1,10,20);
```

The next most common transform is scaling. In the identity matrix, the values that are 1 will scale the element. The first scales it horizontally; the second scales it vertically. If you want to move an element 10 pixels down, 20 pixels to the right, and scale it up by 2, the matrix would look like this:

```
-webkit-transform: matrix(2,0,0,2,10,20);
transform: matrix(2,0,0,2,10,20);
```

3D transforms look a lot more complex, but they're only slightly different. **Figure 7.12** shows the identity matrix for a 3D transform.

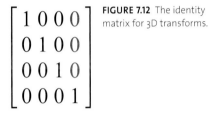

FIGURE 7.12 The identity matrix for 3D transforms.

Again the translate values are highlighted. There are a lot more numbers, but all that's really changed is that there are values for Z, not just X and Y. The 3D version of the same translation looks like this (the lines are broken for clarity and the relevant portions are highlighted):

```
-webkit-transform: matrix3d(2,0,0,0,
                            0,2,0,0,
                            0,0,1,0,
                            10,20,0,1);


transform: matrix3d(2,0,0,0,
                    0,2,0,0,
                    0,0,1,0,
                    10,20,0,1);
```

The Z values are unchanged because the transform we're applying is still really only two dimensional. Actual 3D effects are beyond the scope of this book, but some very cool things can be accomplished.

The beauty of transforms is that they provide a snapshot of the element's state. You can easily keep track of the element with a simple array. If you apply multiple transforms at a time, you can do the math for each and then apply them all together with one matrix—clean and simple.

NOTE: To learn more about the nuts and bolts of matrix transforms, check this book's website for links and details.

WRAPPING UP

Animation is not just eye candy. It is a fundamental part of how modern interfaces are designed. When we talk about gestures later in this book, you'll see how critical they are for giving user feedback.

In this chapter you learned how CSS really speed up animations. You also learned some of the trade-offs between 3D and 2D animation, and how to use `requestAnimationFrame` when you have no choice but to resort to JavaScript animation.

We've talked about speeding up animation. Modern websites end up with a lot of JavaScript as well, and in the next chapter we'll go into detail about how to optimize JavaScript for fast interaction on touch devices.

PROJECT

For this project, use the mock shown in **Figure 7.13**, which displays a list of photo thumbnails.

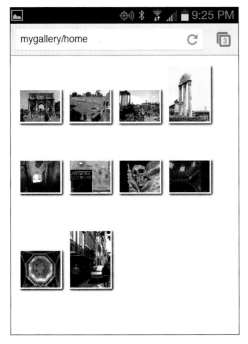

FIGURE 7.13 A photo thumbnail gallery.

Create code so that when the user taps on a thumbnail it zooms up to fill the screen as much as possible and then displays the best possible image when the animation is finished. When the user taps again, the large photo should return to its previous size. Animations should be as smooth as possible.

CHAPTER 8

Maximizing JavaScript Performance

After a while, no matter how careful you are, your client code can still end up unacceptably slow. In this chapter you'll learn how to find these problems and gain some principles to follow when optimizing for touch.

PERFORMANCE TESTING AND DEBUGGING

After World War II several new religions cropped up around the South Pacific. Inspired by the canned food, tools, and other supplies air-dropped by Allied and Japanese forces, indigenous people imitated the behavior of the foreigners, building landing strips, imitation planes, and items of technology. They also practiced military drills as ritual, all in the hope that the cargo would return. These religions are generally referred to as "cargo cults."

A lot of JavaScript performance advice is applied in the same way. Developers use things that they've heard improve performance without understanding what they're doing, why they are doing it, or even if it will help. This chapter will focus on performance ideas specifically related to improving the responsiveness of an interface, but hopefully you will also come away with an appreciation of how important empirical testing is to performance optimization. Browser engines change, devices evolve. Never blindly accept performance tips (even the ones in this book): instrument, test, and validate your assumptions.

THE SCIENTIFIC METHOD

The best way to avoid a cargo cult is to apply science:

- Come up with a question.
- Form a hypothesis.
- Test the hypothesis.
- Review the results.
- Make a conclusion.

    Simple tests can answer most performance problems.

SIMPLE TESTING WITH CONSOLE.TIME()

Testing JavaScript performance is usually a matter of testing how much time it takes to execute. Android Chrome and iOS Safari implement `console.time()`, a method of accurately timing execution in JavaScript. To time something, call `console.time(label)` and then `console.timeEnd(label)` when finished. The console will output the time that passed between both calls, identified by the label.

This is a simple approach to testing, and in most cases it works fine. Sometimes you really want to dig into a performance problem. For those times jsPerf is the ultimate tool.

USING JSPERF FOR PERFORMANCE TESTING

JSPerf.com is a website where you can define test cases, run them in a variety of browsers, and compare the results. It's a very simple yet incredibly powerful tool.

Creating a test with jsPerf.com could not be simpler: navigate to the site, give your test a name and description, add test cases, and start testing. If you have performance problems, isolate the issue, create a test case, and if you want to really dig into the question, use jsPerf.

A few things to keep in mind when using jsPerf:

- The results are only as good as the cases you write. Make sure that you're isolating your variables and testing only one thing at a time.

- You can't use it to compare performance directly between browsers, just the relative performance of your test cases on each browser.

- You can't directly compare tests from different methodologies. If something can't be tested in all browsers with the same system, you can't fully trust the results.

THE WRITE-ONLY DOM

The main reason to write JavaScript on a web page is to interact with the DOM. You want elements to animate, you want values to change. Unfortunately, the DOM is quite slow compared to simple JavaScript. Every interaction you make with the DOM—even *reading* values from it—is going to be expensive.

The following test (http://jsperf.com/dom-vs-cached-value) demonstrates the cost:

```
// 10,372,715 ops/sec on JSPerf
var title = document.getElementById('thisone').title;


// 70,447,551 ops/sec (pre-cached value).
var title = cache['8143594951'];
```

Getting an element by ID and reading a value that isn't affected by styles is a very fast operation in the DOM, yet it still takes seven times as long as getting a value from an object. Getting something more expensive, like offsetHeight is even worse. Using the same test to get offsetHeight rather than title was 56 times slower than getting a value from an object.

CACHING THE DOM

Obviously it isn't possible to completely avoid reading from the DOM, but you can greatly reduce how often you read by caching data smartly. At a minimum you should store any DOM reference in a JavaScript variable if you think you'll need it again. If you need just the value of something from the DOM, store only that. If you update the value in the DOM (changing the position, for example) then update the value in JavaScript at the same time you write to the DOM, you won't have to read again.

Caching is complex, as previously mentioned. But rather than thinking of just one technique, train yourself to watch for superfluous DOM reads. If you find yourself fetching the same value twice from the DOM, you know you should be caching the first fetch. If you set a specific, known value you can also store that, preventing duplicate DOM reads.

For example, in the case of a JavaScript animation that expands the width of an element, you wouldn't want to check the size of the element on each iteration. You can also cache a pointer to the DOM node, so you don't need to fetch it each time (**Listing 8.1**).

LISTING 8.1 Caching DOM values

```
var el = document.getElementById('grow');

//store only the initial value of offset width
var w = el.offsetWidth;

//continue using the original value without returning to the DOM
function render() {
   w = w + 5;
   el.style.width = w + 'px';
}

function loop(){
   if(w < 800) {
      webkitRequestAnimationFrame(loop);
      render();
   }
}

loop();
```

WHY IS THE DOM SLOW?

The work that the DOM does just to find a node is inherently slower than simply retrieving a value from memory. Some DOM operations also require recalculating styles to read *or retrieve* a value. All the offset* values have this problem. Perhaps the biggest problem is that DOM operations are blocking, so when one is in progress nothing else can happen, including the user interacting with the page (except for scrolling, which we'll discuss more later).

PRIORITIZING USER FEEDBACK

As mentioned before: the real secret to perceived performance is user feedback. As you approach JavaScript performance problems, the first priority must be getting out of the way of user feedback. Everything else can wait.

YIELDING

JavaScript in the browser is single-threaded, which means that the JavaScript engine can do only one thing at a time. This thread is the same one that the DOM runs in; it's usually called the UI thread. The appearance of parallelism is achieved by pushing all tasks into a queue, which is executed as the thread becomes idle.

If a slow DOM operation is in progress, incoming events must be queued and handled when that operation is finished. If a slow DOM read is in progress and the user interacts with the page, the events won't be handled right away. This is also true for slow JavaScript tasks, like compiling templates or processing AJAX responses. If the browser is busy, the interface is stuck. A stuck interface is not a good user experience. That's why it's important to prioritize user feedback.

PROCRASTINATING

If the browser is busy giving the user feedback and you need to do something expensive like handle an AJAX response, you can always just procrastinate. Which is to say, schedule the task for later. Set a flag: a simple value that tells the code to schedule itself to try again later (**Listing 8.2**).

LISTING 8.2 Using flag to delay a task

```
var uibusy = false;
function handleResponse(response) {
   if(uibusy) {
      window.setTimeout(function(){
         handleResponse(response)
      }), 100);
   } else {
      //handle response
   }
}
```

Now the response handler will keep trying until there's a good time to do the work.

PUTTING IT TOGETHER: INFINITE SCROLL

Infinite scroll is a UI pattern where content is fetched from the server and appended to the bottom of the page so the user can scroll indefinitely. It's a cool idea and very widely used. It also happens to be quite tricky to get right, particularly from a performance perspective.

For this example you'll create an infinitely scrolling view of slides from a Flickr search, as seen in **Figure 8.1**. (You can reuse the code from earlier examples.)

FIGURE 8.1 An infinitely scrolling list of photos.

TEMPLATES AND CSS FOR THE INTERFACE

Let's start with the markup, as usual. We'll use handlebar templates again, and structure this as a list of <div> elements, each one representing a slide. Each slide will contain an image and a caption. Rather than load the images upfront, we'll defer them and load them as they come into view.

We'll look at how that works shortly, but for now the images will have a single pixel GIF as their src and the real URL will be stored in a data attribute. **Listing 8.3** shows an abbreviated version; download the full sample from the website.

```
<div id="wrapper">

</div>

<script id="slide" type="text/x-handlebars">
   <div id="s-{{id}}" data-id="{{id}}" class="slide">
     <div class="imgholder">
        <a title="by {{ownername}} on Flickr" target="_blank"
        href="http://www.flickr.com/photos/{{owner}}/{{id}}">
        <img class="img" data-src="{{url_n}}" src="/empty.gif" ></a>
     </div>
   </div>
</script>
<script type="text/javascript" src="handlebars.js"></script>
<script type="text/javascript" src="bird_data.js"></script>
<script type="text/javascript" src="scroller.js"></script>
```

The CSS is relatively simple, just designed to turn each image into slides of equal height. The images themselves are sized using max-width and max-height so they fit inside the slide element. There's a transition on the opacity of the image. This is to make the image deferral smoother (**Listing 8.4**).

LISTING 8.4 The markup for infinite scroll styles

```
body {
   margin: 0;
   padding: 0;
   text-align: center;
}

.slide {
   width: 300px;
   padding: 20px;
   margin: 10px auto 10px auto;
   height: 250px;
   background: #f6f6ed;
   position: relative;
   text-align: center;
}
```

```
.slide p {
  width: 100%;
  overflow: hidden;
  white-space: nowrap;
  text-overflow: ellipsis;
  font-family: sans-serif;
}

.slide .img {
  max-width: 100%;
  max-height: 210px;
  text-align: center;
  opacity: 1;
  display: inline;
  -webkit-transition: opacity 0.25s ease-in-out;
  transition: opacity 0.25s ease-in-out;
}

.imgholder {
  width: 100%;
  text-align: center;
}
```

SCRIPTING AN INFINITE SCROLL

To create the infinite scroll effect, you need to determine if the user has scrolled to within a threshold. If so, fetch more content and append it to the page. The distance from the top of the document to the top of the current viewport is in `window.pageYOffset`. If that value is greater than the `offsetHeight` of the body plus the viewport height, you know the user has reached the bottom of the page.

One thing you want to avoid is too much waiting when the user hits the bottom of the loaded content. To avoid that, set a threshold much bigger than the viewport height. That way when the user reaches the bottom of the content, more content should already be loaded (**Listing 8.5**).

LISTING 8.5 Creating an infinite scroll

```
function handleScroll(e) {
  if(window.scrollY + 1000 > document.body.offsetHeight) {
    //get more data and append it
    fetchBirds();
```

```
    }
    handleDefer();
  }
}
window.addEventListener('scroll', handleScroll);
```

The `fetchBirds` function makes a search with the Flickr API and then inserts each response into the DOM using the templates defined earlier (**Listing 8.6**).

LISTING 8.6 Fetching data

```
function fetchBirds() {
  if(fetching) {
    return;
  } else {
    fetching = true;
  }

  window.birdData.fetchPhotos('seagull', page++, function(data) {
    console.time('render');
    var len = data.length;
    for (var i=0; i < len; i++) {
      document.getElementById('wrapper').innerHTML += template(data[i]);
    }
    fetching = false;
    handleDefer();
    console.timeEnd('render');
  });
}
```

NOTE: The rendering block is instrumented with `console.time`. This will be very useful when we try to improve performance on this block later.

The problem with fetching content with lots of images is that as soon as they're inserted into the DOM, the browser will start fetching them. This means that all the simultaneous download slots in the browser will be full, leaving the user watching images slowing appear. Also, because content is loaded ahead of the user, she's forced to download images that she might never see.

The `handleDefer()` function solves this. The `<img>` tags in the template don't actually have the images in their `src` property:

```
<img class="img" data-src="{{url_n}}" src="/empty.gif" ></a>
```

The handleDefer() function loads the real src for the image when it becomes visible. This makes the page faster because fewer downloads happen in the background, and it saves users money and battery life (**Listing 8.7**).

LISTING 8.7 Deferring images

```javascript
function isVisible(node) {
   //get the dimensions we need
   var scrollTop = window.scrollY,
      offTop = node.offsetTop,
      offsetHeight = node.offsetHeight,
      innerHeight = window.innerHeight,
      topViewPort = scrollTop,
      bottomViewPort = scrollTop + innerHeight;

   //figure out if it is in the viewport or not
   return offTop + offsetHeight > topViewPort && offTop < bottomViewPort;
}


function handleDefer() {
   //find all the slides, I'm fetching the container
   //rather than the image because I don't know the image
   //heights yet
   var list = document.querySelectorAll('.slide');
   for (var i=0, len = list.length; i < len; i++) {
      thisImg = list[i].querySelector('.img');
      if(thisImg.src) {
         continue;
      }
      //if they are visible, update the src
      if(isVisible(list[i])) {
         var src = thisImg.getAttribute('data-src');
         if(src) {
            thisImg.src = src;
            thisImg.removeAttribute('data-src');
         }

      }
   }
}
```

This example will work, but it won't work well. On Safari (iPhone) the scrolling is very smooth, but the images seem to all pop in at once when scrolling has stopped. On Android the scrolling frame rate is poor, even when the scroll isn't stuttering. There are lots of performance problems here, but the biggest problem is the scroll handler.

On Android the scroll event is fired repeatedly as the user scrolls—about a hundred times a second on the Galaxy S III. This means that the handleScroll() and handleDefer() functions are also being called hundreds of times, and those are not cheap functions. On Safari the problem is the opposite: the scroll event is fired exactly once each time the user scrolls—as soon as the scroll animation stops. While the user scrolls on the iPhone, none of the code that's supposed to update the interface is even running.

A solution to this problem is to replace the scroll handler with a timer: simply check every 500 ms to see if the user has scrolled (**Listing 8.8**). If he hasn't, do nothing; if he has, call handleShow().

LISTING 8.8 Replacing the scroll event with a timer

```
//cache values so other functions don't need to
//get them again

var lastScrollY = window.pageYOffset,
    //window cache
    scrollY = window.pageYOffset,
    innerHeight,
    topViewPort,
    bottomViewPort;


function handleScroll(e, force) {

   //if scroll hasn't changed, do nothing;
   if(!force && lastScrollY == window.scrollY) {
      window.setTimeout(handleScroll, 100);
      return;
   } else {
      lastScrollY = window.scrollY;
   }

   scrollY = window.scrollY;
   innerHeight = window.innerHeight;
   topViewPort = scrollY -1000;
   bottomViewPort = scrollY + innerHeight + 1000;
```

```
    if(window.scrollY + innerHeight + 2000 > document.body.offsetHeight) {
        fetchBirds();
    }

    handleDefer();
    window.setTimeout(handleScroll, 500);
}

window.setTimeout(handleScroll, 500);

fetchBirds();
```

There's a cache for the window parameters so that other functions (like check visibility) can take advantage of them. This dramatically improves the scrolling performance, both on the iPhone and on devices that fire scroll events normally; both now will only check scroll changes every 100 ms. There's plenty of room left for performance improvement, but there's one last change to make before digging into performance data: the image deferral. Setting the src is technically the best; once the pictures are in view the browser starts fetching the data, streaming it into view. This has the side effect of *feeling* slow. The user is forced to watch images load—watching images paint just seems slower. Instead you can have images fade in once they're fully loaded. It's actually slightly slower, but the experience feels faster.

Modify the handleDefer() function to preload the image rather than load it, and then change the class when loading finishes (**Listing 8.9**).

LISTING 8.9 Deferring animated images

```
/* add the animation to css */
.slide .img {
    -webkit-transition: opacity 0.25s ease-in-out;
    -moz-transition: opacity 0.25s ease-in-out;
    -o-transition: opacity 0.25s ease-in-out;
    transition: opacity 0.25s ease-in-out;
}

/* Update the defer function */
function handleDefer() {
    console.time('defer');
    var i, list, thisImg, deferSrc, img, handler,

    //the slide cache is populated by the function that
```

```
//loads the data so that the defer code doesn't need
//to keep querying the dom.
list = slideCache,
len = listLength;


for (i=0; i < len; i++) {
   thisImg = list[i].img
   var deferSrc = list[i].src;
   if(isVisible(list[i].id)) {

      //create a closure so that the handler
      //function has access to the right data
      handler = function() {
         var node, src;
         node = thisImg;
         src = deferSrc;

         return function () {
            node.src = src;
            node.style.opacity = 1;
            loaded[deferSrc] = true;
         }
      }();

      var img = new Image();
      img.onload = handler;
      img.src = list[i].src;


   }
}
console.timeEnd('defer');
}
```

Now the images will animate as they load. Thanks to CSS animation this animation doesn't slow down the page very much, but the gain in perceived performance is significant—animated loading feels faster.

You might have noticed the other tweak to this function: we're getting the information about the slides from `slideCache` rather than the DOM. This is applying the write-only DOM strategy. The only time the DOM is modified is when new content is appended. Data is cached until needed with the function `updateSlideCache` (**Listing 8.10**).

LISTING 8.10 Caching the slide data

```
var slideCache;

function updateSlideCache(node) {
   var list = node.querySelectorAll('.slide'),
     len = list.length
     obj;

   slideCache = [];

   for (var i=0; i < len; i++) {
     obj = {
        node:list[i],
        id:list[i].getAttribute('data-id'),
        img:list[i].querySelector('.img')
     }

     obj.src = obj.img.getAttribute('data-src');
     slideCache.push(obj);
   }
}
```

The node parameter here is a node containing only the newly added slides. Now the `handleDefer` function is fetching data only from this cache, not directly from the DOM.

Another slowdown point is the `isVisible()` function. In this version about half the time spent in the `handleDefer` function is spent running `isVisible`. It's easy to see why: that function requires a lot of DOM reading and inspection to perform its calculations. Because the position of the slides in the DOM doesn't change, this function is highly cacheable (**Listing 8.11**).

LISTING 8.11 Using caching to quickly check element visibility

```
var slideMap = {};

//to simplify look up this now takes a photo id,
//which is the same as a slide id.
function isVisible(id) {
```

```
        var offTop, offsetHeight, data;

        //if the slide is cached we can get the
        //values from there
        if(slideMap[id]){
            offTop = slideMap[id].offTop;
            offsetHeight = slideMap[id].offsetHeight;

        //if the slide is not cached, update the cache
        }else {
            node = document.getElementById('s-' + id);
            offsetHeight = parseInt(node.offsetHeight);
            offTop = parseInt(node.offsetTop);
            data = {
                node:node,
                offTop:offTop,
                offsetHeight:offsetHeight
            };

            slideMap[id] = data;
        }

        //in the cached case this is just math, no DOM inspection at all
        if(offTop + offsetHeight > topViewPort && offTop < bottomViewPort) {
            return true;
        } else {
            return false;
        }
}
```

After these optimizations, run a few tests. In testing, the defer and scroll code take very little time, with defer now taking between 2 and 20 milliseconds on the iPhone 4. There's one number standing out in the tests though:

```
defer:   20ms
defer:   15ms
render: 1404ms
```

Rendering the new content is taking a long time—over a second. This is enough to cause noticeable jitters in scrolling. The question is why—what's taking so long? Rendering isn't slow, but inserting into the DOM *is* slow. It turns out that adding the string to a node and then appending that node to the DOM is twice as fast. So let's do that instead (**Listing 8.12**).

LISTING 8.12 Optimizing DOM insertion

```
function fetchBirds() {

    //don't refetch if a fetch is in progress
    if(fetching) {
        return;
    } else {
        fetching = true;
    }

    window.birdData.fetchPhotos('seagull', page++, function(data) {
        console.time('render');
        var len = data.length,
        str = '',
        frag;

        for (var i=0; i < len; i++) {
            str += template(data[i]);
        }
        frag = document.createElement('div');
        frag.innerHTML = str;
        document.getElementById('wrapper').appendChild(frag);
        updateSlideCache(frag);
        fetching = false;
        //fire the defer code once to make sure the visible photos
        //load
        handleScroll(null, true);
        console.timeEnd('render');
    });
}
```

After all these optimizations the page feels fast on both the Galaxy S III and the iPhone 4. In the end, only real data answers that question. A simple test (**Table 8.1**) based on the instrumentation on the iPhone shows how much better the optimized code was at rendering and handling the image deferral. Thankfully, the optimized code (**Table 8.2**) was a huge improvement.

TABLE 8.1 Unoptimized performance results

METRIC	MEAN	MEDIAN
Defer	49.2 ms	43 ms
Render	2129.6 ms	2153.5 ms

TABLE 8.2 Optimized performance results

METRIC	MEAN	MEDIAN
Defer	17.1 ms	11 ms
Render	120.5 ms	86 ms

WRAPPING UP

Performance optimization is not rocket science, but it should be approached scientifically. Challenge your assumptions and make decisions based on real data, but be prepared to make things less efficient if it results in a better-perceived experience. Most importantly, get out of the user's way and make feedback your top priority.

PROJECT

Rebuild this chapter's code, this time allowing the user to enter a search term before showing the results. Include the title and description. Make sure that scrolling and loading is smooth.

Then change it so that the infinite scroll is horizontal, rather than vertical.

Lastly, make the horizontal scroll "stick" at each slide. If the user stops scrolling and a slide isn't exactly centered, animate the scroll centering the slide.

CHAPTER 9

The Basics of Gestures

Gestures are what make modern touch interfaces great. They're a big part of why phones and tablets are displacing desktop computers. Great mobile interfaces support gestures.

A gesture is a type of interaction characterized not by a single event, but by a continuous motion made with the fingers. Most gestures simulate manipulation of objects: swiping between photos, scrolling a page, and pinching to zoom. Other gestures don't relate to manipulation at all, and they don't usually give feedback. Those kinds of gestures are more like keyboard shortcuts.

In this chapter we'll focus on the most basic and important gesture: the swipe. This is the one that any good touch interface will need at some point. Swiping is so basic to the touch experience that users expect it to work and they expect it to work seamlessly.

WHY GESTURES?

Gestures aren't as easy as taps because they require some analysis of what has changed over time. IE10 and iOS Safari have limited support for specific gesture events, but for cross-browser support you'll need to implement gestures yourself. Even if the native gestures worked cross-browser they're very limited and won't provide the kind of fine control necessary to give good feedback.

So why even bother? Clicks are good enough on the desktop. The simple answer is that in many cases users will assume gestures work. Certain types of interaction on touch devices are assumed to be swipeable (and zoomable).

CONVENTIONS OF TOUCH INTERFACES

As alluded to in Chapter 1, "The Mobile Landscape," certain conventions of touch interfaces need to be followed. Some interactions require swiping. Most commonly a carousel or slide show must support left and right swiping to make sense in a touch context.

Look at this example from the Yelp review site (**Figure 9.1**). The three images almost beg to be swiped. When users see a row of icons on a mobile site, they tend to expect the control to be swipeable.

In this example from Flickr, the film strip originally had clickable arrows on either side (**Figure 9.2**). But when we observed people using the site on an iPad we saw that most of them tried to swiped the image strip a few times before giving up and trying to tap the arrow targets. Even though there was nothing to indicate that the control could be swiped, users immediately assumed that it could be, because that type of interaction is normally swipeable—a convention of a touch interface.

FIGURE 9.2 The film strip control from Flickr as seen on an iPad.

Beyond the fact that users expect to use gestures, there's another good reason to do so: it's less difficult for users. A swipeable control presents a fairly large and forgiving target, one that's easy to operate with one hand riding the subway. A small tap target is much harder to hit, particularly with the thumb.

PROGRESSIVE ENHANCEMENT AND GESTURES

Gestures are great, no question. But they don't always work. Some browsers, like IE9 for Windows Phone 7, don't support them. Some people don't like them or can't use them. And users who have a mobile screen reader might not be able to interact properly with a swipeable control. So instead of depending on gestures, it's best to build an interface that works without them, then add them as an enhancement to the basic interaction. This approach to web development is known as progressive enhancement.

BUILDING IN LAYERS
Since Netscape 1, web developers have been faced with browsers that vary in their support of new technologies. Rather than have an interface that degrades when those features aren't present, progressive enhancement proposes building up layers on a baseline that will always work.

The original case for progressive enhancement was presented in 2003. At that time browser support for CSS and JavaScript was unreliable. Progressive enhancement proposed creating simple, functional HTML sites with CSS and JavaScript built on top in layers that added functionality. When advanced features failed, the next layer below was available.

On a touch interface, gestures are the top layer. They should be a layer on top of a fully functional JavaScript interface that doesn't depend on gestures. In the next section we'll walk you through the process of building up these layers.

CREATING A PROGRESSIVELY ENHANCED TOUCH CONTROL

Let's say we want to create a web interface for a porch light so the user can turn it off and on from an iPhone. To make sure the light can be turned off and on from less capable user agents, we'll build the control with progressive enhancement in mind. At it's most basic, this interface would be a form that reflected the state of the light (**Listing 9.1**).

LISTING 9.1 Building a power switch control

```
<h1>A Simple Switch</h1>
<h2>Power: <span id="status">OFF</span></h2>
<form action="/power">
   <label for="power">Power:</label>
   <!-- these DIVs don't do anything yet -->
   <div class="switchwrap">
     <div class="switch">
     </div>
     <input type="checkbox" id="power" />
   </div>
   <p><input type="submit" value="Submit" /></p>
</form>
```

Assuming there's some kind of server code to handle the form submission to /power this will do the job. In CSS we turn the <div> tags in the markup into a beautiful little switch, and hide the input button so it's present only for those using a screen reader (**Listing 9.2**).

LISTING 9.2 Exploring the light switch CSS

```
body {
   font-family: sans-serif;
   background: #ccc;
}

/* gradients */
.switchwrap{
   /* cross browser versions omitted for clarity */
   background: linear-gradient(to bottom, #cccccc 0%,#eeeeee 100%);
}
```

```css
.switchwrap .switch {
  /* cross browser versions omitted for clarity */
  background: linear-gradient(to bottom, #b8e1fc 0%,#a9d2f3 10%,
    #90bae4 25%,#90bcea 37%,#90bff0 50%,#6ba8e5 51%,#a2daf5 83%,
    #bdf3fd 100%);
}

form {
  text-align: center;
  width: 150px;
  position: relative;
  margin:auto;
  font-size:18px;
}

input {
  font-size: 18px;
}

/* the js class makes sure these only work if JavaScript is enabled */
.js .switchwrap {
  position: relative;
  width: 150px;
  height:30px;
  margin:auto;
  box-shadow: inset 1px 1px 3px #000, inset -1px -1px 3px rgba(0,0,0,0.3);
  border-radius: 25px;
  overflow: hidden;
}

.js .switchwrap .switch {
  position: absolute;
  top:0;
  left:0;
  font-size: 12px;
  width: 28px;
  height: 28px;
  border: 1px solid #333;
  border-radius: 25px;
```

```
box-shadow: 1px 1px 2px rgba(0,0,0,0.5), inset 1px 1px 1px rgba
   (255,255,255,0.6);
}


/* input hidden off screen so screen readers can still use this control */
.js .switchwrap #power{
   position: absolute;
   top:0;
   left:-1000px;
}
```

The `.js` class exists so those features aren't added for the rare user agent that doesn't support JavaScript. At the top of the page, a short inline script adds that class to activate these styles:

```
<script type="text/javascript">document.body.className = "js";</script>
```

At this point the light switch looks like **Figure 9.3**. None of the controls work, so we need a simple script to toggle the switch upon click (**Listing 9.3**).

FIGURE 9.3
The light switch.

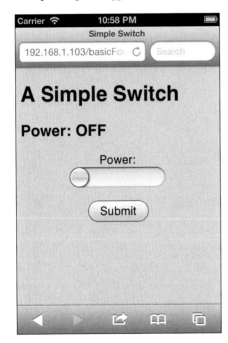

LISTING 9.3 Toggling the light switch

```
var isOn = false;

var $ = function(selector) {
   return document.querySelector(selector);
}

function turnOn() {
   $('#status').innerHTML = 'ON';
   isOn = true;
}

function turnOff() {
   $('#status').innerHTML = 'OFF';
   isOn = false;
}

var theSwitch = $('.switch');

theSwitch.addEventListener('click', function(e) {
   if(isOn) {
      theSwitch.style.left = '0px';
      turnOff();
   } else {
      theSwitch.style.left = '119px';
      turnOn();
   }
});
```

This interface works. We can turn the light on and see the status of the light, and it doesn't look too bad. Unfortunately, on a touch device it feels a little weird because the switch can't be manipulated naturally. It looks like it should be, but instead it's a click interaction. That's fine on a desktop, but on a touch device it feels kind of broken. Instead let's make the switch swipeable.

LISTENING TO TOUCH EVENTS

Now we'll put the touch events to full use. There are four critical events to listen to: touchstart, touchmove, touchcancel, and touchend.

To handle a swipe, we need to determine how far the user's finger has moved since touchstart, then see if it's gone far enough to turn the light on. If the switch moves past the center point of the control, we'll turn the light on.

To add a listener to the four events, it's simplest to use a single function to handle all four, with a `switch` or `if` statement to handle the different events (**Listing 9.4**).

LISTING 9.4 Listening to touch events

```
var TRANSITION_END = 'webkitTransitionEnd',
    TRANSITION_CSS = '-webkit-transition',
    TRANSFORM_CSS = '-webkit-transform',
    TRANSFORM = 'webkitTransform',
    TRANSITION = 'webkitTransition';

//unprefixed
if(document.body.style.transform) {
    TRANSITION_END = 'transitionend';
    TRANSITION_CSS = 'transition';
    TRANSFORM_CSS = 'transform';
    TRANSFORM = 'transform';
    TRANSITION = 'transition';
}

var l = $('form').offsetLeft;

var startLeft;

function handleTouch(e) {

    switch(e.type) {
        case 'touchstart':

            break;
        case 'touchmove':

            break;
        case 'touchcancel':
```

```
        break;
    case 'touchend':

        break;
    }
}


theSwitch.addEventListener('touchstart', handleTouch);
theSwitch.addEventListener('touchend', handleTouch);
theSwitch.addEventListener('touchmove', handleTouch);
```

We need to know where the control starts to calculate where the user's finger is. In this case that is simply the left edge of the form, so we can use the `offsetLeft` property. We'll also need to keep track of where the gesture started. At the top is a very simple way to normalize the APIs.

Another reason to use one function to handle all the events is that it keeps together the logic that defines the gesture. Although there are four events, they really define one thing: the start, middle, and end of a gesture. On `touchstart` we save the starting values for the gesture for later comparison. As `touchmove` events fire we update the display to provide user feedback and keep track of how far the gesture has gone. On `touchend` we clean up the gesture and make sure to handle any snap-back animations.

PROVIDING USER FEEDBACK

This widget is supposed to give the user the feeling of manipulating an actual switch. That means the switch needs to move with the user's finger. This is more realistic, but it also tells the user that the interface has registered the touch and is responding. In addition, if the user moves a finger a little bit to see if she can interact with the control by touch she'll get immediate feedback when she sees the switch move with her finger.

Inside the `touchmove` event we'll move the switch based on the position of the user's finger. This movement has to happen very frequently to give the impression that the switch is always beneath the finger (**Listing 9.5**).

LISTING 9.5 Handling touchmove

```
case 'touchmove':

    //l is the offsetLeft of the form
    goTo = (e.touches[0].pageX - l);

    if(goTo < 119 && goTo > 0) {
        lastX = e.touches[0].pageX - l;
```

```
      //update the position
      theSwitch.style[TRANSFORM] = 'translate3d(' +
      (e.touches[0].pageX - l) + 'px' + ',0,0)';
   }


   if(goTo > 60 && !isOn) {
      console.log('turn on');
      turnOn();
   } else if (goTo < 60 && isOn) {
      console.log('turn off');
      turnOff();
   }


   break;
```

Each time the move event is fired, we need to calculate where the switch should go based on the touch position, then check to see if it's within the widget area (so the switch doesn't fly out of its slot). If it is, we'll move it into the new position with 3D transforms, then check to see if it has crossed the threshold and toggle the switch.

Finally we need to tell the user what happened. If she flipped past the threshold and let go, we'll move the switch all the way to the end. If not, we'll snap it back to its start position.

SNAPPING BACK

What I call "snapping back" is when the interface moves with the gesture but the user releases without triggering the threshold. In this case, rather than pop back to the original position, the return is animated. To make this feel smoother we can apply an ease-out function to the transition. Because the duration is constant, the snap back moves faster the farther it is from the point it started, which will give it a rubbery, springy feeling (**Listing 9.6**).

LISTING 9.6 Handling touchend

```
case 'touchcancel':
//fall through to touchend, logic is the same
case 'touchend':
   if(lastX > 60) {
      endPoint = 119;
   } else {
      endPoint = 0;
   }


   theSwitch.style[TRANSITION] = TRANSFORM_CSS + ' .1s ease-out';
   theSwitch.style[TRANSFORM] = 'translate3d('+endPoint+'px,0,0)';
   break;
```

The touchcancel event is fired when the gesture is interrupted. In this case we want to treat that as if the gesture has ended, so we'll let the touchcancel case fall through. Now the widget should feel quite natural. The switch moves a bit like a real switch and it doesn't behave oddly.

> **NOTE:** This is a simple case of swiping. Another common use is to create a widget where interaction is completely based on gestures. A common one is the lightbox.

BUILDING A TOUCH LIGHTBOX

Lightbox widgets have been standard on the web since the original lightbox.js was released in 2005. A lightbox creates a modal dialog box for viewing large images, typically with Next and Previous buttons to navigate between slides. Probably influenced by the native photo browser on the iPhone, the lightbox experience on mobile typically supports some kind of gestural navigation.

My friends at the bird foundation want a lightbox for a feature on California hummingbirds, and they definitely want it to be a great touch experience.

Because the lightbox is so common on mobile devices, users have a very good idea of what a "fast" lightbox feels like. The most important thing is that the slides move with the user's finger. When the user stops gesturing, the slides should animate into the next position, or snap back if the slide does not advance.

DISABLING NATIVE GESTURES

This lightbox will completely take over the page, based on the assumption that users want to see the photos as large as possible. When creating this kind of interface, precise positioning is very important to keep the illusion of manipulation working. If the user scales the interface using native gestures it will break in weird and frustrating ways. To prevent that we'll add some more values to the viewport meta property.

> **NOTE:** The correct way to support the pinch gesture is by reimplementing it in JavaScript. We'll cover pinch to zoom in Chapter 11, "Pinching and Other Complex Gestures."

```
<meta name="viewport" content="width=device-width,initial-scale=1.0,
  maximum-scale=1.0,user-scaleable=no">
```

CREATING THE THUMBNAIL HTML

Next we'll create a `<div>` that contains an unordered list of thumbnails. We'll use data-properties on the thumbnails to make sure the lightbox has enough information to display the slide.

We'll include `data-full-width` and `data-full-height` with the height and width of the full size image the thumbnail represents. We *could* get this number from the image once it is fetched. But if we have it upfront we can start building the slides without waiting for a server round-trip, resulting in a much faster experience (**Listing 9.7**).

LISTING 9.7 Defining the thumbnail markup

```
<ul>
<li> <!-- each thumbnail looks like this -->
   <a class="slidelink" href="http://www.flickr.com/photos/steveberardi/
     ➝ 7819216372">
      <img data-flickr-url="http://www.flickr.com/photos/steveberardi/
        ➝ 7819216372"
      alt="Black-Chinned Hummingbird"
      data-full-height="495"
      data-full-width="640"
      src="http://farm9.staticflickr.com/8287/7819216372_f189440d20_q.jpg"
      height="75" width="75">
   </a>
</li>
<!-- additional thumbnails follow the same format -->
</ul>
```

STYLING THE THUMBNAILS

Next we'll make the thumbnails prettier and add some other visual flourishes (**Listing 9.8**).

LISTING 9.8 Using lightbox styles

```
html {
   background: #f1eee4;
   font-family: georgia;
   color: #7d7f94;
}


h1 {
   color: #ba4a00;
}
```

```css
.welcome {
   text-align: center;
   text-shadow: 1px 1px 1px #fff;
}

.welcome h1 {
   font-size: 20px;
   font-weight: bold;
}

.welcome {
   -webkit-box-sizing: border-box;
   -moz-box-sizing: border-box;
   box-sizing: border-box;
   margin:5px;
   padding:10px;
   box-shadow: 2px 2px 5px rgba(0,0,0,0.5);
   border-radius: 5px;
}

.carousel {
   margin:5px;
}

.carousel ul li {
   height: 70px;
   width: 70px;
   margin: 5px;
   overflow: hidden;
   display: block;
   float: left;
   border-radius: 5px;
   box-shadow: 1px 1px 2px rgba(0,0,0,0.5), -1px -1px 2px rgba(255,255,255,1);
}

.slidelink {
   display: inline-block;
   height: 75px;
   width: 75px;
}
```

```css
/* This makes the lightbox fill the page with gray */
.slidewrap {
   position: absolute;
   width: 100%;
   overflow: hidden;
   top: 0px;
   bottom: 0px;
   left:0px;
   right:0px;
   background: #444;
   display: none;
}

/* The slide itself fills the viewport */
.slide {
   width:100%;
   height:200px;

   position:absolute;
   text-align: center;
   top:40px;
   left:0px;
}

/* Just a starting point for the image in the slide
   inline styles will replace a lot of this */
.slide div {
   display: inline-block;
   height:100px;
   width:100px;
   background-size:100%;
   background-repeat:no-repeat;
}

.slide .caption {
   display: block;
   position: absolute;
   text-align: left;
   top: 0px;
   left: 0px;
```

```
   width:150px;
   height:25px;
   background:rgba(0,0,0,0.5);
}


.slide .caption a {
   color: #fff;
   text-decoration: none;
   font-family: sans-serif;
}


.controls {
   font-family: arial;
   font-size: 28px;
}


.controls a {
   color: #fff;
   text-decoration: none;
}
```

The visual flourishes are shown in **Figure 9.4**.

FIGURE 9.4 The thumbnail view.

CREATING A BASIC LIGHTBOX

The JavaScript for the lightbox needs to do a few different things:

- Gather the data about the lightbox and initialize.
- Hide and show the lightbox.
- Create the HTML for the lightbox chrome. (What I'm calling the chrome is the interface of the lightbox that isn't the images: the Next and Previous buttons and the gray background.)
- Build the slides.
- Handle touch events.

Because this is a widget rather than an application we don't need to build a separate data layer. Instead we'll extract the data for the widget from the DOM.

BROWSER NORMALIZATION

As before, we need to make things work in every browser (**Listing 9.9**). We'll skip IE10 for now, but go over it in the next chapter.

LISTING 9.9 Using browser normalization code

```
function $(selector) {
    return document.querySelector(selector);
}


var TRANSITION    = 'transition',
    TRANSFORM     = 'transform',
    TRANSITION_END = 'transitionend',
    TRANSFORM_CSS  = 'transform',
    TRANSITION_CSS = 'transition';


if(typeof document.body.style.webkitTransform !== undefined) {
    TRANSITION = 'webkitTransition';
    TRANSFORM = 'webkitTransform';
    TRANSITION_END = 'webkitTransitionEnd';
    TRANSFORM_CSS = '-webkit-transform';
    TRANSITION_CSS = '-webkit-transition'
}
```

UTILITY FUNCTIONS

Instead of typing -webkit-transform and translate3d over and over again, let's create a few utility functions to do the work for us (**Listing 9.10**).

LISTING 9.10 Creating lightbox utility functions

```
function setPosition(node, left) {
   node.style[TRANSFORM] =  "translate3d("+left+"px, 0, 0)";
}

function addTransitions(node){
   node.style[TRANSITION] = TRANSFORM_CSS + ' .25s ease-in-out';

   node.addEventListener(TRANSITION_END, function(e){
      window.setTimeout(function(){
         e.target.style[TRANSITION] = 'none;'
      }, 0)
   })
}

function cleanTransitions(node){
   node.style[TRANSITION] = 'none';
}
```

The lightbox widget will be initialized at page load, even though the user might not request it right away. Because the initialization is fairly light, it will be a better experience if we do it while the user is looking at the thumbnails so the lightbox appears to start instantly.

INITIALIZATION

Because this is a widget, we'll implement it as a constructor. If we want to reuse it, we just need to pass a selector to the constructor (**Listing 9.11**).

LISTING 9.11 The lightbox constructor

```
function Lightbox (selector) {

   var containerNode = $(selector),
      wrapper,
      chromeBuilt,

      currentSlide = 0,
      slideData =[],

      boundingBox = [0,0],

      slideMap = {};
```

```
//call init right away.
init();


return {


  show: show,
  hide: hide
};


}
```

This constructor returns an object. This approach is a way to actually hide inner functions to create true private methods. That way we can expose a simple interface to anyone else who uses this widget.

In the constructor we called a separate init function. We could have done this same work inline with the constructor, but this is cleaner, and keeping these things together in one function can also be helpful for refactoring.

The init function grabs all the `<li>` nodes, finds the thumbnails, and records the information in the slideData array. This array contains all the data we need to manage the slide show. However, because we want this to feel as fast as possible when it launches, we don't want to have to search the entire array when the lightbox opens to find the right slide (the index of this slide won't be present in the event from a tap on a thumbnail). To do that we'll keep an object called slideMap that maps the href of the thumbnail link to the slideData element in the array for faster lookup (**Listing 9.12**).

LISTING 9.12 Initializing the lightbox

```
function init(){
  var slides = containerNode.querySelectorAll('li');
  var thisSlide, thisImg;

  for (var i=0; i < slides.length; i++) {
    thisSlide = {}, thisImg = slides[i].querySelector('img');

    //substitute the large "Z" size image from flickr for the thumbnail
    thisSlide.url = thisImg.getAttribute('src').replace(/_s|_q/, '_z');

    thisSlide.height = thisImg.getAttribute('data-full-height');
    thisSlide.width = thisImg.getAttribute('data-full-width');
    thisSlide.link = slides[i].querySelector('a').href;

    //add to the slidemap.
```

```
            slideMap[thisSlide.link] = slideData.push(thisSlide) - 1;
            thisSlide.id = slideMap[thisSlide.link];
        }
    }
}
```

At this point the lightbox is ready to go. The rest of the initialization happens in the show function (**Listing 9.13**).

LISTING 9.13 Showing the lightbox

```
    function show(startSlide){
        if(!chromeBuilt){
            buildChrome();
            attachEvents();
        }
        wrapper.style.display = 'block';
        boundingBox = [ window.innerWidth, window.innerHeight ];

        goTo(slideMap[startSlide]);
        attachTouchEvents();
    }
```

BUILDING THE CHROME

The buildChrome function creates the HTML wrapper for the lightbox and sets chromeBuilt to true so the lightbox chrome doesn't get rebuilt each time the user hides or shows the lightbox. We'll create template functions but we won't use any real templating language because these templates are so simple it isn't really necessary (**Listing 9.14**).

LISTING 9.14 Building the chrome

```
var wrapperTemplate = function(){
    var div = document.createElement('div');
    div.innerHTML = '<div class="controls">'+
    '<a class="prev" href="#">prev</a> | '+
    '<a class="next" href="#">next</a></div>'+
    '</div>';
    div.className = "slidewrap";
    return div;
}

function buildChrome(){
    wrapper = wrapperTemplate();
```

```
document.body.appendChild(wrapper);
boundingBox[0] = wrapper.getAttribute('offsetWidth');
chromeBuilt = true;
}
```

The last step in building the chrome is attaching an event handler for the Next and Previous links (**Listing 9.15**).

LISTING 9.15 Handling clicks

```
function handleClicks(e){
  var target = e.target;

  //prevent default is only called when conditions match
  //so that clicks to external resoures (like Flickr) work.
  if(target.className == 'next') {
    e.preventDefault();
    goTo(currentSlide + 1);
  } else if(target.className == 'prev'){
    e.preventDefault();
    goTo(currentSlide - 1);
  } else if (target.className != 'flickr-link') {
    e.preventDefault();
    hide();
  }
}

function attachEvents(){
  wrapper.addEventListener('click', handleClicks);
}
```

Now the lightbox chrome is ready for some actual slides. In the show function we call goTo() to load the starting slide. This function shows the slide identified by the parameter, but it will also lazily build the slides as we need them.

NOTE: Don't name a function goto in all lowercase. goto is a reserved word in JavaScript.

BUILDING THE SLIDES

When the lightbox opens, the slide the user requested is in the viewport and the previous and next slides are to the left and right. When the user clicks (or swipes) Next, the current slide moves off to the left and the next slide moves into position (**Figure 9.5**).

FIGURE 9.5 A slide in the lightbox. © AnnCam/Flickr. Made available under a Creative Commons Attribution license.

We'll follow the same template approach we used for the wrapper and create a slide-Template function. The function accepts the slide data object we built in the init function (**Listing 9.16**).

LISTING 9.16 Creating a slide template

```
function slideTemplate(slide){
    var div = document.createElement('div');
    div.className = 'slide';
    div.innerHTML = '<div style="background-image:url('+slide.url+')">'+
    '<div class="caption"><a class="flickr-link" href="'+slide.link+'">
    → By '+slide.owner+' on Flickr</a></div>'+
    '</div>';
    return div;
}
```

We're using a `<div>` rather than an `<img>` to force the browser to render a smaller image when handing it off to the GPU. (This approach was discussed in depth in Chapter 7, "CSS Transitions, Animation, and Transforms.") This makes things much faster and reduces the memory footprint.

The buildSlide function itself is more complex. In addition to pushing the slide data through the slide template, the code also has to make sure that the slide fits in the viewport. A scale factor is determined by finding out how much bigger the largest slide is than the available space. Once a scale factor is found, the image is scaled and the slide appended to the DOM (**Listing 9.17**).

LISTING 9.17 Building the slide

```
function buildSlide (slideNum) {

  var thisSlide, s, img, scaleFactor = 1, w, h;

  //make sure to not build slides with no data for them
  if(!slideData[slideNum] || slideData[slideNum].node){
    return false;
  }

  thisSlide = slideData[slideNum];
  s = slideTemplate(thisSlide);

  img = s.querySelector('div');

  //image is too big! scale it! (using the bounding box data
  //I recorded in the init function
  if(thisSlide.width > boundingBox[0] || thisSlide.height > boundingBox[1]){

    if(thisSlide.width > thisSlide.height) {
      scaleFactor = boundingBox[0]/thisSlide.width;
    } else {
      scaleFactor = boundingBox[1]/thisSlide.height;
    }

    w = Math.round(thisSlide.width * scaleFactor);
    h = Math.round(thisSlide.height * scaleFactor);
    img.style.height = h + 'px';
    img.style.width = w + 'px';
```

```
    }else{
        img.style.height = thisSlide.height + 'px';
        img.style.width = thisSlide.width + 'px';
    }

    thisSlide.node = s;
    wrapper.appendChild(s);
    setPosition(s, boundingBox[0]);
    return s;
}
```

MOVING THE SLIDE INTO POSITION

The goTo function moves the requested slide and adjacent slides into position. In the event that the requested slide is not the next or previous slide, this code will move it into position first before animating (**Listing 9.18**).

LISTING 9.18 Using the goTo function

```
function goTo(slideNum){

    var thisSlide;

    //failure, return to last slide
    if(!slideData[slideNum]){
        goTo(currentSlide);
    }

    if(Math.abs(currentSlide - slideNum) !== 1 &&
    slideData[currentSlide] && slideData[currentSlide].node){
        //current slide not adjacent to new slide!
        setPosition(slideData[currentSlide].node,
        (slideNum < currentSlide)  ? boundingBox[0] : 0 -  boundingBox)
    }

    thisSlide = slideData[slideNum];

    //build the adjacent slide
    buildSlide(slideNum);
    buildSlide(slideNum + 1);
    buildSlide(slideNum - 1);
```

```
//animate the slides entering and leaving
if(thisSlide.node){
   addTransitions(thisSlide.node);
   setPosition(thisSlide.node, 0);
}

//previous slide exists, move it away
if(slideData[slideNum - 1] && slideData[slideNum-1].node){
   addTransitions(slideData[slideNum - 1 ].node);
   setPosition( slideData[slideNum - 1 ].node , (0 - boundingBox[0]) );
}

//next slide is ready, animate it into position
if(slideData[slideNum + 1] && slideData[slideNum + 1].node){
   addTransitions(slideData[slideNum + 1 ].node);
   setPosition(slideData[slideNum + 1 ].node, boundingBox[0] );
}

currentSlide = slideNum;
}
```

At this point the lightbox is more or less functional. We can go to the next and previous slide. We can hide and show. It would be ideal to know when the user reaches the first or last slide, maybe by graying out the controls. This lightbox is usable on a desktop or a touch device.

ADDING GESTURE SUPPORT

Most touch devices include a native photo viewer. These various apps, following the original iPhone photos app, have created a UI convention: a swipe to the left advances the slide. Several implementations of this interaction give no feedback at all; the slides simply advance when the gesture is completed.

The best approach is to give live feedback. As the user swipes, the slide moves under the user's finger and the next (or previous) slide appears to the left or right. This gives the illusion that the user is pulling along a strip of photos—manipulating the interface (**Figure 9.6**).

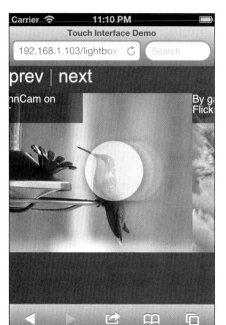

FIGURE 9.6 Swiping between slides.

LISTENING FOR TOUCH EVENTS

Many libraries include support for touch events. In general I don't recommend using them. When handling touch events you are updating an element live as the user gestures. Any delay at all will be immediately obvious to a user: it will *feel* slow. Adding a layer of indirection will necessarily affect performance, that's why I've avoided libraries throughout this book.

Because this interface takes over the screen we won't listen for touch events just on the slide. Ideally users shouldn't have to work to find touch targets, so we'll listen for touch events on the root node of the DOM—a swipe anywhere on the screen will work.

As in the previous example, we'll use the same function to handle all the touch events (**Listing 9.19**).

LISTING 9.19 Attaching touch events

```
function attachTouchEvents() {

    var bd = document.querySelector('html');
    bd.addEventListener('touchmove', handleTouchEvents);
    bd.addEventListener('touchstart', handleTouchEvents);
    bd.addEventListener('touchend', handleTouchEvents);

}
```

HANDLING TOUCH EVENTS

I created three variables to maintain state during the gesture. These will contain the starting point of the gesture and the last position of the gesture (startPos and endPos, respectively). The complete function is contained in **Listing 9.20** on the website, but we'll step through it here because it's fairly complicated.

The touchstart event fires at the beginning of any touch event, so it will record where the gesture started. Make sure to clean off any transitions that might have been left on the nodes. If transition styles are set to a node it won't move immediately, but via a transition. This would kind of ruin the effect of the gesture feedback (Listing 9.20).

LISTING 9.20 Using the handleTouchEvents function

```
//going left or right?
var direction = 0;

if(e.type == 'touchstart'){
   startPos = e.touches[0].clientX;
   lastPos = startPos;
   direction = 0;
   if(slideData[currentSlide] && slideData[currentSlide].node){
      cleanTransitions(slideData[currentSlide].node);
   }

   if(slideData[currentSlide + 1] && slideData[currentSlide + 1].node){
      cleanTransitions(slideData[currentSlide + 1].node);
   }

   if(slideData[currentSlide - 1] && slideData[currentSlide -1].node){
      cleanTransitions(slideData[currentSlide -1].node);
   }
}
```

In the touchmove we'll find out how much the touch has moved along clientX, and then move the current slide the same amount. If the slide is moving to the left, you also move the next slide. If it's moving to the right, move the previous slide instead. That way we only ever move two nodes, but we give the illusion that the whole strip is moving. Having a map to the slide information lets us do all of this without doing any more DOM reads, only writes.

```
if(e.type == 'touchstart'){
/*..*/
} else if(e.type == 'touchmove'){
   e.preventDefault();
   //if the last position is bigger than the starting position, the
   //gesture is moving right
   if(lastPos > startPos){
      direction = -1;
   }else{
      direction = 1;
   }

   //Move the currently visible slide with the gesture, as well as
   //the next or previous, depending on the direction
   if(slideData[currentSlide]){
      setPosition(slideData[currentSlide].node, e.touches[0].clientX
      ➥ - startPos);
      if(direction !== 0 && slideData[currentSlide + direction]){
         if(direction < 0){
            setPosition(slideData[currentSlide + direction].node,
               (e.touches[0].clientX - startPos) - boundingBox[0]);
         }else if(direction > 0){
            setPosition(slideData[currentSlide + direction].node,
               (e.touches[0].clientX - startPos) + boundingBox[0]);
         }
      }
   }

   //record the last position
   lastPos = e.touches[0].clientX;

}
```

When the touch ends, the code needs to decide whether to advance, go back, or do nothing. If the answer is do nothing, the slides need to snap back into position, giving the user feedback as to why the slide didn't change. We won't stop moving the slide if it's the last one, we'll just snap back. This makes it clear to the user that the interface hasn't frozen, but the end has been reached (**Figure 9.7**). We actually accomplish this in the goTo function in the previous listing. When we pass slideNum to goTo, it simply recurses and returns to the same slide.

FIGURE 9.7 Reaching the end of the slides.

```
else if(e.type == 'touchend'){
   if(lastPos - startPos > 50){
      goTo(currentSlide-1);
   } else if(lastPos - startPos < -50){

      goTo(currentSlide+1);
   }else{

      //snap back!
      addTransitions(slideData[currentSlide].node);
      setPosition(slideData[currentSlide].node, 0);

      if(slideData[currentSlide + 1] && slideData[currentSlide + 1].node){
         addTransitions(slideData[currentSlide + 1]);
```

```
        setPosition(slideData[currentSlide + 1].node, boundingBox[0]);
    }

    if(slideData[currentSlide - 1] && slideData[currentSlide - 1].node){
        addTransitions(slideData[currentSlide - 1]);
        setPosition(slideData[currentSlide - 1].node, 0 - boundingBox[0]);
    }

}

}
```

This lightbox is obviously a simple example of using gestures. But the concept remains the same: tell the user a story about what's happening all the time. With transitions and animations, you can show the user what the interface is doing with continuous feedback.

WRAPPING UP

As you build mobile web interfaces, you'll find yourself using swipe gestures a lot. They really are one of the fundamental building blocks of a good touch interface. As long as you keep in mind the goal of continuous feedback, you'll probably be successful.

The examples in this chapter didn't do a lot of processing outside of displaying the interface. The second example made a point of doing the necessary processing before the user tapped on the thumbnails, making sure that work didn't get in the way of providing immediate user feedback.

In the next chapter you'll get more details on swipes, as well as more information on the swipe's close relative, scrolling.

PROJECT

Build on the example in this chapter and Chapter 8, "Maximizing JavaScript Performance," to create a widget that lets users swipe through the results of a Flickr search.

- Use a set list of photos to get it started, snapping back at the end of the list.
- Change it so the results are continuous until there are no more from the Flickr API.
- Add code to prune the old nodes so there are never more than three slide nodes on the page.

CHAPTER 10

Scrolling and Swiping

Few things on touch interfaces are as unpleasant as broken or slow scrolling and swiping. In this chapter we'll go into more depth about how to make an interface with both. The goal is to make it fast, lightweight, and most importantly, to make it feel right. You'll learn about scrolling with swiping, and get details on making touch events work in Internet Explorer 10 for Windows 8.

SCROLLING

Scrolling with one finger is the most common user gesture. It's also one that's easy to ignore because usually you don't have to worry much about it—if your page is tall enough, scrolling will just work itself out. In the layout shown in **Figure 10.1** and **Figure 10.2** the designer wants the image to stay fixed with the text scrollable, and he wants the user to be able to swipe between pages. In this layout scrolling will not take care of itself.

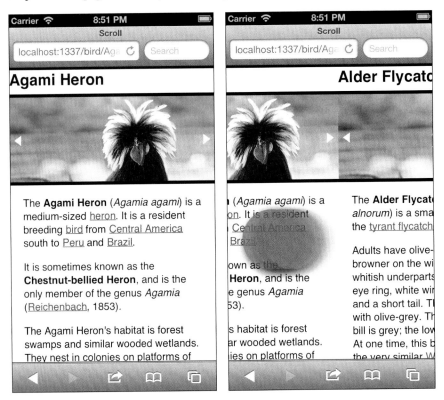

FIGURE 10.1 The mock-up for a bird information browser. The designer used a photograph of a chicken to represent a generic bird.

FIGURE 10.2 How swiping will work in this interface.

NATIVE SCROLLING

Browsers are really good at scrolling. Even old, slow Android devices are snappy when scrolling a static page. Users have a very good sense of how scrolling should feel. When it doesn't feel exactly right users will notice. If scrolling feels broken, the whole site will feel broken.

Simple native scrolling on iOS 5+, Android 3+, and IE10 is easy: `overflow:auto` works on elements just as it does on the desktop (with some minor issues we'll talk about later in this chapter).

On Android 2.3.x the native browser does not support `overflow:auto` at all. In that browser scrolling of individual elements is not natively supported. That might not be so bad considering the operating system is two years old. Unfortunately, according to Google, fifty percent of Android users are still using Android 2.3.x.

You can build this layout in all the major browsers without resorting to JavaScript. Rather than using a scrollable `<div>` you can use fixed positioning.

For fixed positioning to work properly on Android, the viewport meta property must include `width=device-width` and `user-scalable=no` (**Listing 10.1**).

LISTING 10.1 Bird browser markup

```
<!-- Some head content omitted for clarity -->
<head>
<meta name="viewport" content="width=device-width, user-scalable=no">
</head>
<body>
<div class="view">

  <div class="slide">

    <div class="header">
      <h1 class="title">Acorn Woodpecker</h1>

      <div class="hero">
        <div class="navigation">
          <a href="{{prev.path}}" title="Previous Bird"
            class="prev-link arrow">
            <span>◀</span>
          </a>
          <a href="{{next.path}}" title="Next Bird"
            class="next-link arrow">
            <span>▶</span>
          </a></div>
        <img class="hero-img" src="/images/chicken.jpg">
      </div>

  </div>
```

```
<div class="bd">
   <p>content...</p>
</div>

   </div>

</div> </body>
```

This example uses UTF-8 characters for the arrows. When possible this is a great option to reduce the size of the page. One small consideration: using a triangle in this context might be confusing for screen reader users. A screen reader will read these links as "right-pointing triangle" and "left-pointing triangle." To make this more accessible, you could add a WAI-ARIA label to the `<a>` element, for example : `aria-label="next photo"` would tell screen readers that the link is not only a right-facing triangle, but also a link to the next photo. CSS for this page will adapt to fit the various screen sizes it's faced with (**Listing 10.2**).

LISTING 10.2 CSS for a position:fixed layout

```
body * {
   /* easier math */
   -webkit-box-sizing:border-box;
   -moz-box-sizing:border-box;
    box-sizing:border-box;
}

body {
   font-family: sans-serif;
}

.header {
   height: 178px;
   position: fixed;
   overflow: hidden;
   width: 100%;
   top: 0;
   left: 0;
   border-bottom: 5px solid black;
   background: #fff;
}

.hero {
   display: block;
```

```css
    position: relative;
    height: 85%;
    width: 100%;
    padding-top: 5px;
    text-align: center;
    background: #000;
}

/* the links each cover half of the photo,
to allow click/tap navigation */
.navigation {
    position: absolute;
    top: 0px;
    left: 0px;
    width: 100%;
    height: 100%;
    padding: 0;
    margin: 0;
}

.navigation .arrow {
    color: #fff;
    text-decoration: none;
    position: absolute;
    height: 100%;
    width: 50%;
}

.navigation .arrow span {
    display: block;
    position: absolute;
    top: 40%;
    left: 5px;
}

.navigation .next-link {
    left: 50%;
}
```

```
.navigation .next-link span {
  left: auto;
  right: 5px;
}

/* The image scales to fit the element, up until it hits
its native width or height */
.hero-img {
  display: inline;
  max-height: 100%;
  max-width: 100%;
}

.title {
  border-top: 4px solid black;
  color: black;
  height: 40px;
  font-size: 24px;
  width: 100%;
  margin: 0;
  text-align: left;
}

/* the body has a top margin big enough
to make room for the header */
.bd {
  width: 100%;
  margin-top: 210px;
  padding: 0px 20px;
}
```

The key to this layout is highlighted: the main content has a top margin big enough to accommodate the header, and the position of the header is fixed. This layout displays wonderfully in all major mobile browsers, including Android 2.3.

If the designer had called for a fixed footer we would just need to make sure that the bottom of the content has enough extra space so text is not obscured when the user scrolls to the bottom.

The only problem with this approach is that the scroll bar will fill the height of the screen, rather than just the height of the element being scrolled (**Figure 10.3**).

FIGURE 10.3 The scroll bar in the center of the page (pictured here in Android 2.3).

HANDLING OVERFLOW:AUTO

In some cases overflow:auto may be the only option. This works as well as native scrolling on Android 3+ and IE10. On iOS overflow:auto is different from native scrolling. Normally scrolling on iOS has momentum: when you let go, the scroll continues and then slows down as if you flicked it. Scrollable elements, by default, don't do this; they stop moving as soon as you remove your finger. To fix this there's a prefix CSS property in WebKit: adding -webkit-overflow-scrolling: touch; to a selector will add native-style scrolling in iOS, with momentum. Android and Windows Phone 8 don't have this problem and they safely ignore the -webkit-overflow-scrolling property.

OVERFLOW IN ANDROID 2

In Android 2.3 and below, overflow:auto is treated like overflow:hidden. That means that if your design requires overflow:auto, half of Android users won't be able to scroll the element natively. If you feel Android 2.3 support is required and there's no room to change the design, you'll have to reimplement scrolling in JavaScript.

Don't try to re-implement native scrolling if you can avoid it. It's not possible to perfectly replicate native scrolling. It doesn't help that devices running older operating systems are also generally much slower, where using JavaScript to move an element will probably not perform anywhere near as well as native scrolling. Anything less than perfection will be immediately noticeable to the user as "something wrong" with the site.

Warnings aside, it's quite possible to create a reasonable approximation of native scrolling with touch events. The simple idea is to put another element within the scrolling element and then move the inner element along with a swipe gesture. In reality things can get quite complex. Instead of trying to reinvent the wheel, you can use either Overthrow (github.com/filamentgroup/Overthrow) or iScroll 4 (cubiq.org/iscroll-4), both of which solve the problem quite well.

ADDING OVERFLOW WITH OVERTHROW

Overthrow is a polyfill, which means that rather than reimplementing scrolling, it attempts to implement the feature on older browsers while leaving the native behavior untouched on new browsers.

To use it, simply include overthrow.js, add the class "overthrow" to the element that will scroll, and everything will work. On browsers that need a polyfill, it won't work quite as well as native, but it will work well enough and it's quite seamless (**Listing 10.3**).

LISTING 10.3 Using Overthrow

```
<!DOCTYPE HTML>
<html lang="en-us">
<head>
    <meta http-equiv="Content-Type" content="text/html;charset=UTF-8">
    <meta name="viewport" content="width=device-width">
    <meta name="viewport" >
    <style type="text/css">
    /* The developers recommend putting .overthrow-enabled in front of
       this, but it isn't necessary and will result in a possible flash
       of content without any overflow at all, as well as introducing
       a dependency on overthrow for _new_ browsers */
       #scrolly {
           width: 200px;
           height: 300px;
           overflow: auto;
           border: 2px solid red;
       }
    </style>
    <script src="/overthrow.js"></script>
</head>
<body>
    <div class="overthrow" id="scrolly">
        <p>Content...</p>
    </div>
</body>
```

OVERFLOW WITH ISCROLL 4

iScroll 4 is a different beast entirely. Rather than a polyfill, iScroll is a full-featured widget that does more than just fix scrolling. The end result is very nice—even on iOS 6 the experience is very nearly as good as native.

The size of the feature set is the reason I normally would not use iScroll 4 unless I needed several of the features it defines. The less you use external libraries the better.

iScroll is a little more complex than Overthrow. The element with the feature applied must have one child node that you intend to scroll. Also, for scrollbars to work properly, the element must have positioning, which is to say that it must have the position property in CSS defined as something other than `inherit`. That's because for iScroll to position the child node properly, it needs to do it relative to the parent node. If the parent node does not have positioning, the child node will be positioned relative to the next parent that has positioning, resulting in unpredictable behavior (**Listing 10.4**).

LISTING 10.4 Using iScroll

```
<html lang="en-us">
<head>
   <meta http-equiv="Content-Type" content="text/html;charset=UTF-8">
   <meta name="viewport" content="width=device-width, user-scalable=no">
   <style type="text/css">
   #scrolly {
      position: relative;
      height: 250px;
      margin: auto;
      width: 90%;
      border: 1px solid red;
   }
   </style>
   <script src="/iscroll.js"></script>
</head>
<body>
   <div id="scrolly">
      <div id="scroller">
         <p>content</p>
      </div>
   </div>
</body>
<script type="text/javascript">
var myScroll = new iScroll('scrolly');
</script>
</html>
```

The result is a scrollable <div> that looks and behaves more or less the same in all browsers (including desktops). It even creates iOS-style scroll bars, which look nice but might be slightly jarring on Android devices (**Figure 10.4**). The performance is acceptable in older Android devices but it's noticeably slower than native scrolling and the problem gets worse as the contents of the element get more complex.

FIGURE 10.4
An iOS-style scroll bar on Android 2.3.

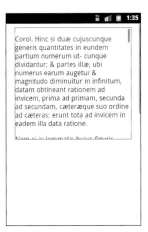

WHEN LAYOUTS FAIL

Mobile layouts can be frustrating. Just when you think you have it completely dialed in, you hand it to somebody and he rotates the phone, completely breaking everything. Or she pinches and zooms in, only to find the whole site suddenly unusable. Getting things working in all these situations is a large part of the challenge of mobile development. In the case of the Birds of California site there are a few issues we haven't handled at all, specifically zooming and orientation changes.

ORIENTATION CHANGES

In landscape orientation this interface is effectively unusable (**Figure 10.5**). When reading content users don't often rotate their phones, but they always can and you don't want your interface to completely break when that happens. The simplest solution is to use media queries to adapt the layout for different orientations. For the landscape orientation we'll move the header over and turn it into a sidebar, leaving the main content scrollable.

The technique for fixed positioning is the same in the new orientation. At the bottom of the style sheet we'll include some overrides inside a media query targeting orientation: landscape (**Listing 10.5**).

FIGURE 10.5 The interface completely breaks in landscape orientation.

LISTING 10.5 Orientation media queries

```
@media screen and (orientation: landscape) {
    .header {
    width: 33%;
    height: 110px;
    border-bottom: 2px solid black;
    }
    .header .hero {
    background: transparent;
    }
    .header .title {
    height: 34px;
    font-size: 14px;
    }
    .header .arrow span {
    top: 10px;
    }

    .bd {
    width: auto;
    margin: 0 10px 0 34%;
    padding: 0px;
    font-size: 12px;
    }
}
```

The result is an interface that looks pretty good in either orientation and switches smoothly between them (**Figure 10.6**).

FIGURE 10.6
Landscape orientation on IE10 for Windows Phone 8.

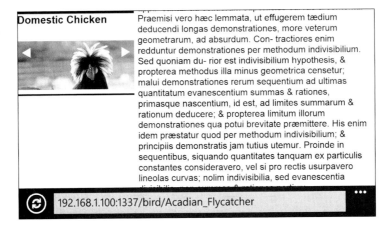

There's another common way layouts can break spectacularly, particularly on iOS: zooming.

ZOOMING

Fixed positioning and zooming don't play well together. On Android, fixed positioning doesn't work at all if zooming is enabled. Windows 8 and iOS attempt to zoom the entire page with unpredictable results (**Figure 10.7**). Effectively if you intend to use fixed positioning, you must add user-scalable=no to your viewport meta property. If you're not using fixed position and are depending on overflow for scroll, zooming is possible but it might not work the way you expect.

FIGURE 10.7 The result of zooming in on the fixed layout in iOS.

As implemented in all the devices I've tested, native zooming always zooms the entire page, never just one element. If you've put content inside a scrollable area the user can zoom in on it, but he can't zoom just that element. Also, once the user has zoomed in, scrolling is naturally difficult as the browser tries to distinguish between panning the page and zooming the element. To have an element that can be zoomed individually you must implement that behavior on your own. We'll cover that in the next chapter.

MAKING THE BIRD BROWSER SWIPEABLE

The concept for this browser is a way to navigate through a list of around 800 bird species scraped from Wikipedia. (The code for the scraper is on this book's website if you're interested.) I turned the list into a large JavaScript array that will serve as the data for this application. Rather than using templating and a data API, we'll build it with HTML fragments for simplicity.

On the server I'm running a Node.js application to serve the data, but it would work just as well with static content. Conceptually there are two endpoints:

- `/bird/birdname`
- `/fragments/birdname`

The fragments contain the full HTML for the bird except HTML head content.

The design for the bird browser showed users swiping between pages. The concept is similar to the lightbox in the previous chapter. When the page opens, we'll build the next and previous bird pages and keep them hidden until the user starts swiping, when we'll show the next or previous page depending on the swipe direction.

Using fixed positioning along with swiping pages is not really feasible. If we use that approach, adjacent pages will end up scrolled to the same position. To achieve the swiping version, we'll need to use `overflow:auto` on fixed positioned elements. The example shown in **Listing 10.6** will not work properly in Android 2.3.

LISTING 10.6 Absolute positioned styles

```
body * {
  -webkit-box-sizing: border-box;
  -moz-box-sizing: border-box;
  box-sizing: border-box;
}

body {
  font-family: sans-serif;
  width: 100%;
  -ms-touch-action: none;
}
```

```css
.slide {
  position: absolute;
  overflow: hidden;
  top: 0;
  left: 0;
  width: 100%;
  height: 100%;
  margin: 0;
}

.header {
  height: 50%;
  overflow: hidden;
  width: 100%;
  top: 0;
  left: 0;
  position: absolute;
  border-bottom: 5px solid black;
  background: #fff;
}

.hero {
  display: block;
  position: relative;
  height: 100%;
  width: 100%;
  padding-top: 5px;
  text-align: center;
}

.navigation {
  position: absolute;
  top: 0px;
  left: 0px;
  width: 100%;
  height: 100%;
  padding: 0;
  margin: 0;
}
```

```css
.navigation .arrow {
    color: #fff;
    text-decoration: none;
    position: absolute;
    height: 100%;
    width: 50%;
}
.navigation .arrow span {
    display: block;
    position: absolute;
    top: 40%;
    left: 5px;
}
.navigation .next-link {
    left: 50%;
}
.navigation .next-link span {
    left: auto;
    right: 5px;
}


.hero-img {
    display: inline;
    max-height: 100%;
    max-width: 100%;
}


.title {
    border-top: 4px solid black;
    color: black;
    height: 40px;
    font-size: 24px;
    width: 100%;
    margin: 0;
    text-align: left;
}
```

```
.bd {
  width: 100%;
  height: 50%;
  position: absolute;
  overflow: auto;
  -webkit-overflow-scrolling: touch;
  top: 50%;
  padding: 0px 20px;
}

@media screen and (orientation: landscape) {
  .header {
  width: 33%;
  height: 110px;
  border-bottom: 2px solid black;
  }
  .header .hero {
  background: transparent;
  }
  .header .title {
  height: 34px;
  font-size: 14px;
  }
  .header .arrow span {
  top: 10px;
  }

  .bd {
  width: auto;
  height: 100%;
  top: 0;
  margin: 0 10px 0 34%;
  padding: 0px;
  font-size: 12px;
  }
}
```

With the styles ready to go we can move on to the fun part: the JavaScript.

BUILDING THE DATA MODEL

To make this application as responsive as possible, we'll emit the entire bird list onto the page. Information about all 800 birds is only 17 KB gzipped. There is some upfront cost, but it will really speed things up. A faster solution would be to give all the birds sequential IDs, but that is often not feasible.

The data is as a list:

```
[
  {
    "latin": "Empidonax virescens",
    "path": "/bird/Acadian_Flycatcher",
    "name": "Acadian Flycatcher"
  },
  {
    "latin": "Melanerpes formicivorus",
    "path": "/bird/Acorn_Woodpecker",
    "name": "Acorn Woodpecker"
  }
]
```

To turn this data into something useful to the application, we'll create an object to manage the list, which will serve as a model. The object will encapsulate the array, but it will also keep a lookup table to speed searches for birds by name, useful if we decide to expand this to a full, single-page application.

The model is implemented using the module pattern because it's a single object that will only be that way once. The performance cost is small and there's great benefit in exposing a clean API (**Listing 10.7**).

LISTING 10.7 The bird data model

```
var birds = (function() {

  var currentBird,
    myBirdList,
    currentBird,
    myBirdList = birdList,
    birdMap = {};
```

The init function will convert the array into an object. Using an object is much faster because there's no need to search through the array to find a particular bird.

```
function init() {
    for (var i=0, len = myBirdList.length; i < len; i++) {
        birdMap[myBirdList[i].name] = i;
    }

    setBird(thisBird);
}


// Find out about the bird at the index
function getInfo(index) {
    return myBirdList[index];
}

function nextBird() {
    return myBirdList[currentBird + 1];
}

//find out about the bird offset items away
function birdAtOffset(offset) {
    return myBirdList[currentBird + offset];
}

//get the current bird
function getThisBird() {
    return myBirdList[currentBird];
}

function prevBird() {
    return myBirdList[currentBird - 1];
}
```

The setBird function sets the current bird to keep track of state. The prevBird and nextBird functions are based on the bird set here.

```
function setBird(birdname) {

    //if it is a path or underscore version
```

```
    if(birdname.indexOf('_') !== -1) {
        //sometimes it might have the /bird/ in front of it
        //but this thing won't care
        matches = birdname.match(/(?:\/bird\/)?(.+)/);
        birdname = matches[1].replace('_', ' ');
    }

    currentBird = birdMap[birdname];
}


return {
    init:init,
    nextBird:nextBird,
    prevBird:prevBird,
    thisBird:getThisBird,
    birdAtOffset:birdAtOffset,

    advance:function() {
        if(myBirdList[currentBird + 1]) {
            currentBird++;
        }
    },

    setBird:setBird
}
}());
```

Next we'll create a wrapper function for data calls to allow inserting a caching layer (**Listing 10.8**). You can see the actual cache implementation in the full example on the book's web page.

LISTING 10.8 Creating a wrapper for data calls

```
function getBirdData(path, callback) {
    path = path.replace('/bird/', '/fragments/');
    var data = modelCache.get(path);

    if(data) {
        /* Timeout 0 makes sure this is asynchronous */
        window.setTimeout(function(){
```

```
        callback && callback(data);
      }, 0);
      return;
    }

    /* Calls the same AJAX implementation I've used before */
    makeRequest(path, function(xhr) {
      modelCache.set(path, xhr.responseText);
      callback && callback(xhr.responseText);
    })
}
```

The next problem to solve is how to handle the pages themselves. Navigation requires a simple way to move the page into the position, create, and destroy it. We'll also want some way to be notified when transitions are over. Because we'll be creating these many times, the prototypical approach will be the fastest. We'll label "private" methods and properties with an underscore (**Listing 10.9**).

LISTING 10.9 The slide class

```
/* Utility functions/browser normalization */
function $(selector) {
    return document.querySelector(selector);
}

var TRANSITION  = 'transition',
    TRANSFORM    = 'transform',
    TRANSITION_END = 'transitionend',
    TRANSFORM_CSS = 'transform',
    TRANSITION_CSS = 'transition';

if(typeof document.body.style.webkitTransform !== undefined) {
    TRANSITION = 'webkitTransition';
    TRANSFORM = 'webkitTransform';
    TRANSITION_END = 'webkitTransitionEnd';
    TRANSFORM_CSS = '-webkit-transform';
    TRANSITION_CSS = '-webkit-transition'
}

/*
 * id is the unique DOM idea
```

```
* content is the html that this slide represents
* and the selector is used in the case that the slide
* content is already on the page
*/
function Slide(id, content, selector) {

   this.id = id;

   this.content = content;

   this._listeners = [];

   this.selector = selector;
   this._build();
}


/*
 * register a listener to be notified when the
 * transition is over
 */
Slide.prototype.onMoveEnd = function(callback) {
   this._listeners.push(callback);
}
```

It will be important to know when the slide is finished changing. This simple observer implementation handles that use case.

Next the _build function (the underscore indicates that it's a private method) encapsulates the work that needs to be done to actually insert the new slide into the DOM.

```
Slide.prototype._build = function(){

   var myNode, that, div;

   if(this.selector) {
      this.node = $(this.selector);
   } else {
      div = document.createElement('div');
      div.innerHTML = this.content;
      this.node = div.querySelector('.slide');
      document.querySelector('.view').appendChild(this.node);
```

To make things faster, we'll insert the content into a document fragment (the `<div>`) rather than appending it directly to the DOM.

```
        }

    this.node.id = this.id;
    myNode = this.node;
    that = this;
    this._handler = this.node.addEventListener(TRANSITION_END, function(e){
        if(!that || !that._listeners) {
            return;
        }
        var i;
        myNode.style[TRANSITION] = '';
        moving = false;
        for (i=0; i < that._listeners.length; i++) {
            if(typeof that._listeners[i] == "function") {
                that._listeners[i]();
            }
        };
    });
}


Slide.prototype.setLeft = function(left) {

    this.node.style[TRANSFORM] = "translate3d(" + left + 'px,0,0)';
}

Slide.prototype.moveTo = function(pos) {
    this.node.style[TRANSITION] = TRANSFORM_CSS +' .2s ease-out';
    this.node.style[TRANSFORM] = "translate3d("+pos+"px,0,0)";
}

Slide.prototype.cleanTransitions = function() {
    this.node.style[TRANSITION] = '';
}
```

```
Slide.prototype.hide = function() {
   this.node.style.display = 'none';
}

Slide.prototype.show = function() {
   this.node.style.display = 'block';
}

/* remove from the DOM. This will also allow the garbage collector
 * to clean up listeners
 */
Slide.prototype.destroy = function() {
   this._listeners = [];
   if(this.node.parentNode) {
      this.node.parentNode.removeChild(this.node);
   }
}
```

This class cleanly encapsulates the task of creating and manipulating the pages and makes sure to clean them up when they're no longer needed.

Because we've got good caching in place and creating slides is very fast (3–10 ms on a fast device, less than 50 on a quite slow device) we're only ever going to keep three pages around: the current page, the next page, and the previous page. Let's call them nextSlide, prevSlide, and currentSlide. Doing this greatly reduces the memory footprint of the site. That makes it faster and prevents it from crashing in low-memory situations.

While the user swipes you really want to focus on the feedback for that interaction. However, a lot of work needs to be done to make sure the user can actually swipe between slides. This work is done in the prepare function that will be called at the end of the transition, when the user is probably not doing anything but looking at the current slide (**Listing 10.10**).

LISTING 10.10 Preparing the slides for interaction

```
var currentSlide, nextSlide, lastSlide,
moving = false,
THRESHOLD = 100,
nextSlide,
prevSlide;

function prepare() {
```

First, we need to ask the data layer if there is in fact a next and previous bird. If there is, we need to make sure we have the data for the slides; we also need to make sure both are constructed and in position.

```
var nextBird = birds.nextBird(),
    prevBird = birds.prevBird();

//make a slide if we can and we haven't already
if(nextBird && (!nextSlide || nextSlide.id !== nextBird)) {
    getBirdData(birds.nextBird().path, function(resp) {
        nextSlide = new Slide(birds.nextBird().name, resp);
        nextSlide.hide();
        nextSlide.setLeft(window.innerWidth);
    });

} else if(!nextBird) {
    nextSlide = false;
}

//same for the previous
if(prevBird && (!prevSlide || prevSlide.id != prevBird)){
    getBirdData(birds.prevBird().path, function(resp) {
        prevSlide = new Slide(birds.prevBird().name, resp);
        prevSlide.hide();
        prevSlide.setLeft(-window.innerWidth);
    });
} else if (!prevBird){
    prevSlide = false;
}
}
```

This function will also run at the beginning to set everything up for the first slide. Now we can create the goTo function that navigates between pages (**Listing 10.11**). The goTo function takes a direction integer and moves to the next or previous slide as requested. In each case we'll add a callback to onMoveEnd to do the cleanup work and the call prepare, effectively waiting for interactions to be over before doing any work that isn't related to user feedback.

LISTING 10.11 Implementing the goTo function

```
function goTo(direction) {
   moving = true;

   if(direction == 1) {
      //when the moving is done, move on to the next slide,
      //saving object where possible.
      currentSlide.onMoveEnd(function(){
         //we don't need this anymore
         currentSlide.destroy();
         prevSlide = currentSlide;
         currentSlide = nextSlide;
         birds.advance();
         prepare();
      });

      currentSlide.moveTo(0 - window.innerWidth);
      nextSlide.moveTo(0);

   } else {

      currentSlide.onMoveEnd(function(){
         currentSlide.destroy();
         currentSlide = prevSlide;
         nextSlide = currentSlide;
         birds.goBack();
         prepare();
      });

      currentSlide.moveTo(window.innerWidth);
      nextSlide.moveTo(window.innerWidth);
      prevSlide.moveTo(0);

   }

}
```

Now that everything's in place, it's time to initialize the interface and start listening for touch events (**Listing 10.12**).

LISTING 10.12 Initializing the application

```
//The first slide
currentSlide = new Slide(thisBird, false, '.slide');
prepare();

document.addEventListener('touchstart', handleTouch);
document.addEventListener('touchmove', handleTouch);
document.addEventListener('touchend', handleTouch);

//prime the cache
birds.birdAtOffset(-2) && getBirdData(birds.birdAtOffset(-2).path);
birds.birdAtOffset(2) && getBirdData(birds.birdAtOffset(2).path);
birds.birdAtOffset(3) && getBirdData(birds.birdAtOffset(3).path);
```

At this point you've probably noticed that we haven't actually created a `handleTouch` function yet. In the last chapter's lightbox we added a touch event handler to the document root. Here we have a bit of a problem. If we did what we did in the previous chapter we would break the scrolling. That's because scrolling is the default event on `touchMove`, so calling `preventDefault(e)` in the event handler will in fact prevent scrolling from happening.

We *could* add the listener just to the header element. The problem with that is that we're constantly creating and destroying the header, so we'd need to continually remove and attach event listeners, greatly increasing the complexity of the code.

Instead we'll check the touch events to see if they originate from the scrollable area and stop handling them if they do (**Listing 10.13**).

LISTING 10.13 Handling touch events

```
function isLink(element) {
    return getAncestor(element, 'A');
}

function getAncestor(element, tag) {
    if(!element.tagName || !tag) {
        return false;
    }
    if (element.tagName == tag) {
        return element;
    } else if(element.tagName !== 'BODY'){
        return getAncestor(element.parentNode, tag);
```

```
    } else {
       return false
    }
}

var lastPos, startPoint;

function handleTouch(e) {
    var diff, anchor, direction = 0, bd;

    if(moving) {
       return;
    }

    //if the target is inside the scrollable area,
    //stop handling events
    bd = getAncestor(e.target, 'DIV');
    if(bd && bd.className == 'bd') {   nextSlide.hide();
       return;
    } else {
       e.preventDefault();
    }

    switch (e.type) {
       case 'touchstart':
          startPoint = e.touches[0].pageX;

          //make sure transitions are cleaned off
          currentSlide.cleanTransitions();

          //show the hidden slides
          if(nextSlide) {
             nextSlide.cleanTransitions();
             nextSlide.show();
          }

          if(prevSlide) {
             prevSlide.cleanTransitions();
```

```
        prevSlide.show();
      }

    lastPos = e.touches[0].pageX;
    break;

case 'touchmove':
    e.preventDefault();
    diff = e.touches[0].pageX - startPoint;

    //move all three slides together
    currentSlide.setLeft(diff);
    if(diff > 0) {
        prevSlide && prevSlide.setLeft(diff - window.innerWidth);
    } else {
        nextSlide && nextSlide.setLeft(diff + window.innerWidth);
    }

    lastPos = e.touches[0].pageX;
    break;

case 'touchcancel':
case 'touchend':
    diff = lastPos - startPoint;

    //if the swipe was very short,
    //and on an anchor, assume it was a tap
    if(Math.abs(diff) < 5) {
        anchor = isLink(e.target);
        if(isLink(e.target)) {
            window.location = anchor.href;
        }
    }

    //figure out if we are advancing,
    //going back or going nowhere
    if(diff < -THRESHOLD && nextSlide) {
        goTo(1);
    }else if (diff > THRESHOLD && prevSlide) {
```

```
            goTo(-1);
        } else {
            //snap back if we are going nowhere
            currentSlide.moveTo(0);
            nextSlide.moveTo(window.innerWidth);
            prevSlide.moveTo(-window.innerWidth);
        }
        break;
    }
}
```

Everything works: we can swipe between bird pages and scroll the text. Except when the orientation changes, the threshold we've defined is too large: the landscape version has a much smaller touch target. What we'll do is change the threshold when the orientation changes.

In touch browsers the device orientation is available in the window.orientation property. Its value is 0 if the device is in portrait orientation and 90 or -90 if it's in landscape orientation. We can check this value when the orientation changes by listening to the orientationchange event.

```
window.addEventListener("orientationchange", function(){
    if(window.orientation !== 0){
        THRESHOLD = 25;
    } else {
        THRESHOLD = 100;
    }
});
```

This event does not reliably fire on all Android devices, as I've learned through experience. Some Android devices fire a resize event only on the change; others fire the event late. Thankfully, they all seem to set the value properly. An orientation change event can then be simulated with a little extra code. We'll create a function that checks whether the orientation has changed, adding it as an event listener to both orientationchange and resize. Then, for devices that fail to fire events correctly for orientation changes, we'll call the checking function every two seconds, just to be sure (**Listing 10.14**).

LISTING 10.14 Handling orientation in all browsers

```
var previousOrientation = 0;
function checkOrientation(){
    //don't bother changing this if the orientation is the same.
    if(window.orientation !== previousOrientation){
        previousOrientation = window.orientation;
        if(window.orientaiton !== 0) {
```

```
        THRESHOLD = 25;
      } else {
        THRESHOLD = 100;
      }
    }
};


window.addEventListener("resize", checkOrientation);
window.addEventListener("orientationchange", checkOrientation);


//as a final fallback, poll.
setInterval(checkOrientation, 2000);
```

MICROSOFT POINTER EVENTS

These touch handlers won't work in IE10 on Windows 8. Even though pointer events are quite different, they actually map quite well to standard touch events. To get this working in IE10, the first thing to do is add -ms-touch-action: none; to the <body> element to override the default operating system gestures. Then we'll add handlers for the MSPointer events (**Listing 10.15**).

LISTING 10.15 Listening to MSPointer Events

```
document.addEventListener('MSPointerDown', handleTouch);
document.addEventListener('MSPointerMove', handleTouch);
document.addEventListener('MSPointerCancel', handleTouch);
document.addEventListener('MSPointerUp', handleTouch);
```

We'll use the same function to handle the pointer events to try and reduce duplicated logic. That means we need to make some changes to make the same function work with both (**Listing 10.16**).

LISTING 10.16 Handling pointer and touch events

```
function handleTouch(e) {

  var diff, anchor, direction = 0;

  if(moving) {
    return;
  }

  //if the target is inside the scrollable area,
```

```
//stop handling events
if(getAncestor(e.target, 'DIV').className == 'bd') {
   nextSlide.hide();
   return;
} else {
   e.preventDefault();
}

switch (e.type) {
   case 'MSPointerDown':
   case 'touchstart':

      startPoint = e.touches ? e.touches[0].pageX : e.screenX;
      currentSlide.cleanTransitions();
      if(nextSlide) {
         nextSlide.cleanTransitions();
         nextSlide.show();
      }
      if(prevSlide) {
         prevSlide.cleanTransitions();
         prevSlide.show();
      }
      lastPos = e.touches ? e.touches[0].pageX : e.screenX;
      break;
   case 'MSPointerMove':
   case 'touchmove':
      e.preventDefault();

      diff = e.touches ? e.touches[0].pageX - startPoint :
      ➥ e.screenX - startPoint;

      currentSlide.setLeft(diff);
      if(diff > 0) {
         prevSlide && prevSlide.setLeft(diff - window.innerWidth);
      } else {
         nextSlide && nextSlide.setLeft(diff + window.innerWidth);
      }
      lastPos = e.touches ? e.touches[0].pageX : e.screenX;
      break;
```

```
    case 'MSPointerUp':
    case 'MSPointerCancel':
  case 'touchcancel':
  case 'touchend':
    //unchanged
    break;
  }
}
```

By checking for the existence of the touches array, we can find out if there even is a pointer or touch event and modify how we get the values we need. Amazingly, there are no other changes required to support IE10—not as difficult as it could be. Microsoft also provides higher-level gesture events (as does iOS Safari). Both implementations are quite different. If a higher-level gesture API does become more standardized it will be useful, but for now I recommend using simple touch (or pointer) events.

WRAPPING UP

In this chapter you learned how to use fixed positioning to create smaller scrollable areas and you discovered some of the benefits and pitfalls of using overflow: auto on smaller elements. You learned about using touch events to handle more complex swipeable interaction, and how to use pointer events to support IE10.

Most touch devices have only one input: the touch screen. Making a working interface demands making interaction with just one finger as simple as possible. The code in this chapter may have seemed quite complex, but I wrote it with the outcome in mind. I also had a touch device in hand to continuously test not only the code, but also the feel of the interface. If you focus on the result—a smooth and responsive interface—you'll find that the code comes naturally.

In the next chapter we'll handle much more complex gestures, particularly multi-touch gestures.

PROJECT

Create a phone-target page with an embedded image carousel above scrollable content. The text should fill the bottom two-thirds of the page, but the top should have ten or so images that the user can swipe between (**Figure 10.8**).

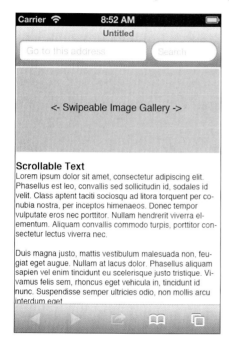

FIGURE 10.8 A mock-up for the project.

For an additional challenge, take the interface you created in this chapter and make the text area also swipeable separately, so a user can navigate between text sections and images individually. Make sure that scrolling continues to work.

CHAPTER 11

Pinching and Other Complex Gestures

Support for multiple touches was one of the "wow" demos Steve Jobs gave when he introduced the iPhone. It's still a pretty cool feature, and it makes touch devices a lot more fun to use.

Handling multi-touch gestures isn't simple. Getting it right requires math and a solid understanding of asynchronous programming in JavaScript. But when you need it, you need it.

In this chapter we'll cover the basics of handling multiple touches in WebKit, Firefox, and Internet Explorer 10. And you'll learn how to implement pinch to zoom, the multi-touch gesture you're most likely to need.

UNDERSTANDING MULTI-TOUCH LIMITATIONS AND SUPPORT

Here's the bad news first: Android 2.3 and below support only one touch in the browser. Although some vendors support multiple touches at the OS level on Android 2.3, it is not available from JavaScript and not usable. Based on the usage numbers this probably means that you can't require multiple touches for your site. Instead you can consider multi-touch as another layer of enhancement on top of touch events.

BROWSER SUPPORT FOR MULTI-TOUCH

Multi-touch is supported in iOS Safari, Android 3 and up, Firefox mobile, Android Chrome, and IE 10. All but IE10 have roughly the same API as well.

MULTI-TOUCH IN IOS

In iOS Safari the touch array can contain up to eleven touches. Because Safari on iOS was the first browser to support multi-touch, other browser touch APIs are either based on or inspired by this interface. The API is the same in every version of iOS that's out so it can be considered quite stable.

Safari also has higher-level gesture events that handle the math of dealing with rotation and scaling. These are available only in iOS and don't really offer enough to be worth using, in my opinion.

MULTI-TOUCH IN ANDROID

Android has supported multiple touches since Android 3. The API is identical to that of iOS, except that there are additional properties of the touch object that might be available if they're supported by the hardware.

NOTE: For more information about touch object properties, see Table 6.2 in Chapter 6, "Taps vs. Clicks: Basic Event Handling."

MULTI-TOUCH IN IE10

IE10 supports multiple touches, but rather than an array of touches for each event, a separate event is created for each touch. IE also has a higher-level gesture API similar to the one in Safari. It's a little more complex, but it also has some powerful features, including an API for inertia animation. Again, it works only in IE10 on Windows 8, so it's of limited utility.

HANDLING MULTIPLE TOUCHES

When dealing with multi-touch, I like to think of each touch having its own life cycle. Regardless of the browser, a touch is born when the user puts her finger on the screen, it lives as she moves it, and it dies when she takes her finger off the screen. Many individual events are fired when this happens, but it helps to think of the individual touch as a constant, even though the objects themselves do not persist between events. For the next example we'll create a debugging tool that will draw circles around each touch point and make it work on Android 3+, iOS Safari, Firefox, and IE10.

LAYING THE GROUNDWORK

First things first: we need to disable as many native gestures as possible. For Android and iOS, we'll add width=device-width, user-scalable=no to the viewport meta property. For IE10 we'll add -ms-touch-action: none; to the body tag. The touched class turns the <div> into a circle (**Listing 11.1**).

LISTING 11.1 Styling the circles

```
<meta http-equiv="Content-Type" content="text/html;charset=UTF-8">
<meta name="viewport" content="width=device-width, user-scalable=no">
<style type="text/css">
   body {
      -ms-touch-action: none;
   }

   .touched {
      /* a box 100px square with a 50px border radius is a circle */
      height: 100px;
      width: 100px;
      border: 1px solid red;
      border-radius: 50px;
      position: absolute;
      top:0;
      left:0;
      opacity:0;
   }
</style>
```

To make this example clearer we'll encapsulate the code for the circle inside a MyTouch constructor (**Listing 11.2**). This object will manage the life cycle of the circles, as well as abstract setting their position.

NOTE: We're using the same browser abstraction code we used in the last chapter.

LISTING 11.2 Creating an object for circles

```
//manage the circles on the page
var touches = {};

function MyTouch(id) {
    this.id = id;
    var touchee = document.createElement('div');
    touchee.className = 'touched';
    touchee.style.opacity = 0;
    touchee.id = id;
    touchee.addEventListener(TRANSITION_END, function() {
        touchee.style[TRANSFORM] = '';
    });

    document.body.appendChild(touchee);
    this.node = touchee;
}

MyTouch.prototype.setPos = function(posX, posY) {

    this.node.style.opacity = 1;
    var x = Math.round(posX - 50) + 'px';
    var y = Math.round(posY - 50) + 'px';
    this.node.style[TRANSFORM] = "translate3d(" + x + "," + y + ",0)"

}

MyTouch.prototype.destroy = function(cb) {
    this.fade();
    var node = this.node, id = this.id;
    window.setTimeout(function() {
```

```
      node.parentNode && node.parentNode.removeChild(node);
      delete(touches[id]);
   }, 1000);


}


MyTouch.prototype.fade = function() {
   this.node.style[TRANSITION] = 'opacity .5s ease-in-out';
   this.node.style.opacity = 0;


}
```

Each circle will have a unique identifier we can use to keep track of it and make sure it stays under the same finger. All the various implementations of touch events provide unique identifiers for touches to make this possible.

To make sure the circles go away when they're no longer needed, we'll create a function to kill them (**Listing 11.3**).

LISTING 11.3 Creating life cycle functions

```
function kill(id) {
   touches[id] && touches[id].destroy();
}


function reaper() {
   var id;
   for (id in touches) {
      kill(id);
   }
}
```

MANAGING THE START OF A TOUCH

In every browser but IE10, a touch is born in a touchstart event. This is where we'll create the touch objects that will draw the circles. The difference between this and previous touch handlers in this book is that in this case we want to loop through the touches array and create a circle for every touch. We'll also do a little checking to make sure we're not recreating a touch that already exists.

For this example (**Listing 11.4**), we'll handle each event separately, rather than using the switch approach we discussed before. This is for clarity, and just to show you another way to handle things.

LISTING 11.4 Handling touchstart

```
document.addEventListener('touchstart', function(e){
    e.preventDefault();
    var len = e.touches.length, thistouch;
    for (var i=0; i < len; i++) {
        thistouch = e.touches[i];

        touches[thistouch.identifier] = new MyTouch(thistouch.identifier);
        touches[thistouch.identifier].setPos(thistouch.pageX, thistouch.pageY);
    }
});
```

Notice that we're using the `identifier` property of each touch object as a key in the touches object. This lets us keep track of the circle during its life cycle. The code will work, unchanged, in iOS Safari, Android 3+, Android Chrome, and Firefox Mobile.

To make the same thing happen with pointer events in IE10 is a little different, because IE creates a separate event for each touch (**Listing 11.5**).

LISTING 11.5 Handling MSPointerDown

```
document.addEventListener('MSPointerDown', function(e){
    touches[e.pointerId] = new MyTouch(e.pointerId);
    touches[e.pointerId].setPos(e.clientX, e.clientY);
});
```

The information about the touchpoint is on the event, rather than a separate touch object. The same information is available, so outside of the event-handling code we don't need to change anything.

ACTING ON TOUCH MOVEMENTS

While the touch is alive, it fires touchmove (or MSPointerMove) events as it moves. Because we're tracking each event's unique identifier we can move the circles with the touch smoothly. The code (**Listing 11.6**) is very similar to the code we used for the start events, except this time we just need to see if we're already tracking that particular touch, based on its identifier. In the non-IE world, we'll loop through the touches and check their identifiers before applying the transformation.

LISTING 11.6 Handling touchmove

```
function mover(e) {
    e.preventDefault();
    var len = e.touches.length,
        thistouch;
    for (var i = 0; i < len; i++) {
```

```
        thistouch = e.touches[i];
        if (!touches[thistouch.identifier]) {
            touches[thistouch.identifier] = new MyTouch(thistouch.identifier);
        }
        touches[thistouch.identifier].setPos(thistouch.pageX, thistouch.pageY);
    }
}
document.addEventListener('touchmove', mover);
```

The code for this is very similar to touchstart. In many cases you can actually combine them into the same function (that would work here; the full example on the website uses that approach)

Again, in the IE 10 version (**Listing 11.7**) everything is basically the same except there is no loop required.

LISTING 11.7 Handling MSPointerMove

```
function moverMS(e) {
    if(!touches[e.pointerId]) {
        touches[e.pointerId] = new MyTouch(e.pointerId);
    }
    rescue(e.pointerId);
    touches[e.pointerId].setPos(e.clientX, e.clientY);
}
```

MANAGING THE END OF THE TOUCH LIFE CYCLE

The final part of the touch life cycle is its death. The touchend event (**Listing 11.8**) doesn't have any touches, but it does have a list of changedTouches, which we'll use to identify which circles to kill.

LISTING 11.8 Handling touchend

```
var reap;

function touchend(e) {
    window.clearTimeout(reap);
    for (var i=0; i < e.changedTouches.length; i++) {
        kill(e.changedTouches[i].identifier);
    }

    //kill any stray touches that don't get cleaned
    reap = window.setTimeout(reaper, 100);
}
```

```
document.addEventListener('touchend', touchend);
document.addEventListener('touchcancel', touchend);
```

In this example the reaper function is called on a timeout. When handling this many touch events I've found that sometimes a touch identifier never appears in the changed-Touches array. The reaper makes sure to remove any strays when the user is idle.

Once again, the Microsoft version is simpler, but basically the same (**Listing 11.9**).

LISTING 11.9 Handling MSPointerUp

```
function touchendMS(e) {
    window.clearTimeout(reap);
    kill(e.pointerId);

    //kill any stray touches that don't get cleaned
    reap = window.setTimeout(reaper, 100);
}

document.addEventListener('MSPointerUp', touchendMS);
```

That's a pretty cool demo. But that's the easy part—implementing multi-touch gestures is extremely difficult. In the next section you'll learn how to handle a pinch, one of the most common multi-touch gestures.

HANDLING PINCHES

Pinching comes naturally on multi-touch devices. It isn't as obvious as swiping, but once you've tried it a couple of time it makes sense. It's built into most mobile browsers, so users expect to be able to zoom into an element they are interested in to see more detail. Like scrolling, pinching is a gesture you don't often have to worry about for that reason. If your layout is complex, or requires fixed positioning, native pinch to zoom can break your layout until the user reloads. The only workaround is re-implementing the pinch gesture yourself, and you're going to have to use math.

THE PINCH EFFECT

It's fairly easy to get a scale factor from touchpoints. In WebKit there's a scale value on the touch event. IE10 gives you scale using gestures.

Once you have a scale factor you can apply it as a transform to the element you want to scale on touch move, creating what I call "naïve" scaling. But it won't feel right. The goal of gestures is to give the impression of manipulating an object. With the naïve approach, the scale effect happens independently of the gesture.

Normally, when you scale an object, it scales around its center. In CSS transforms this is known as the `transform-origin`. By default this is the center of the object (**Figure 11.1**).

To give the proper effect, the image should scale around the center of the touchpoints. That is, the `transform-origin` should be the average of the two touchpoints (**Figure 11.2**).

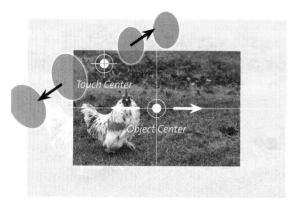 

FIGURE 11.1 With "naïve" scaling, the image scales around its center, regardless of the touchpoints.

FIGURE 11.2 Scaling the image around the touch center, rather than the object center.

THE TRANSFORM-ORIGIN

In CSS you can change the `transform-origin`. This is really handy, for example, if you're rotating an element in CSS: you can turn it around a corner of the element to easily create and position vertical text. Unfortunately, you can't actually use this to solve the pinch to zoom problem.

Setting the transform origin *does* approximate the effect, but it starts to behave strangely as you zoom in. Transform origin is defined in integer values relative to the original position of the element. If the element is 100 pixels by 100 pixels, the transform origin values must be between one and 100. When you try to position the origin, you can place it only as close as the nearest pixel vertex at the original scale—the position is rounded to the nearest integer. Rounding a value introduces a slight error that grows as the scale factor grows.

The end result is that as the image scales it starts to slide around under the touchpoint—not a great experience. So how do you scale an object around a different center point without moving the transform origin? You need to do the same things transforms do, but on your own.

DILATION: A SHORT GEOMETRY LESSON

The next section is not completely necessary to understand and implement zooming, but it is helpful. Feel free to skip ahead to "Implementing pinch to zoom" if you'd rather not slog through the math.

On a coordinate plane, like a browser window, points are represented as an ordered pair of numbers, where the first number represents the *x* position and the second represents the *y* position. In normal notation, points are represented by capital letters. In geometric terms, a rectangle (like a DOM node) is called a polygon. A rectangle is defined by four points, so a rectangle can be identified by its points: polygon ABCD is the rectangle defined by vertices A, B, C, and D (**Figure 11.3**).

FIGURE 11.3
A rectangle defined by its vertices.

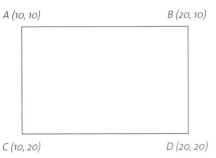

A (10, 10)   B (20, 10)

C (10, 20)   D (20, 20)

In geometry, scaling a polygon is called *dilation*. Dilation is moving the points in a polygon in such a way that the shape of the polygon is not changed. Assuming that you're scaling around the origin point of the coordinate plane, dilation is a simple matter of multiplying each point by a scaling factor:

Let any given point be $X_{(a,b)}$, the scaled point be $Y_{(a, b)}$, and the scaling factor be k.

$$X_a = kYa$$

So given vertex A(10,20), and a scaling factor of 1.5, the resulting vertex would be B = (10*1.5, 20*1.5) = (15, 30). It turns out, however, that this is a simplification of the true dilation. Dilation can also be described as translating the points along rays (a ray is a line that is finite in one direction) that intersect the origin and each of the vertices (**Figure 11.4**).

What you want to do in the pinch case is scale around a different center: the center of the touchpoints. Geometrically speaking, this means defining a new center of dilation to scale from. Rather than drawing the rays from the origin, you draw them from the center of dilation (**Figure 11.5**).

To achieve this, let any point be $X(a,b)$, the scaled point be $Y(a,b)$, the center of dilation be $C(a,b)$, and the scaling factor be k.

$$Y_a = C_a + k(X_a - C_a)$$
$$Y_b = C_b + k(X_b - C_b)$$

This equation gives you the new location of the dilated polygon. We'll be using this to handle pinch to zoom.

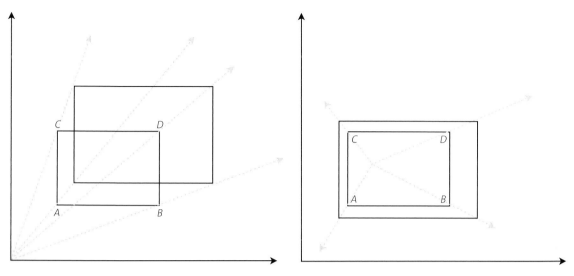

FIGURE 11.4 Scaling a polygon from the origin.

FIGURE 11.5 Scaling from a different center of dilation.

IMPLEMENTING PINCH TO ZOOM

Even with the math squared away this is no picnic. We'll go through the simplest possible implementation here, but in real life you'll need to spend a lot of time dealing with the special cases in your particular application.

CREATING THE LAYOUT

First you'll need a starting point, a page with an image on it that you can zoom. For simplicity's sake, the design shown in **Figure 11.6** has an image right in the middle of the page, with the address bar hidden.

FIGURE 11.6 An image ready for zooming.

This layout is deceptively simple. Continuing with the theme of things that are difficult to do, centering an image nicely in the viewport, with no address bar, is a bit of a challenge.

Centering elements vertically in CSS has always been hard. For this example we'll use JavaScript to do the heavy lifting, but the groundwork is plain CSS and HTML. The HTML is about as simple as possible (**Listing 11.10**).

LISTING 11.10 The HTML for pinch to zoom

```
<!DOCTYPE HTML>
<html lang="en-us">
<head>
   <title>pinchy</title>
   <meta http-equiv="Content-Type" content="text/html;charset=UTF-8">
   <meta name="viewport" content="width=device-width,initial-scale=1,
    ⇥ maximum-scale=1,user-scalable=no">
</head>
<body>
   <div id="holder">
      <div id="img">
      </div>
   </div>
</body>
</html>
```

A few more values are added to the viewport `meta` property here, because it's extremely important that native zooming be disabled in all cases—otherwise it will interfere with the gesture you're trying to create. Adding `initial-scale` and `max-scale` prevents the browser from opening scaled. The style sheet is also about the simplest in this book so far, just adding a holder element to draw the green border, giving a background to the element you'll be scaling and making sure the start values are correct.

In the CSS, the <body> has a large height value (**Listing 11.11**). That's because hiding the address bar requires scrolling, which won't work if the document is too short. Calculating the correct height to make sure this always works is problematic, particularly because there's no reliable way to determine how tall the address bar is in all devices. The safe thing to do is set a body size high enough to guarantee scrolling. Because scrolling will be disabled anyway, this won't affect the interface.

The element to be scaled, #img, has a transform origin set to 0, 0, overriding the default, which is the center of the element.

LISTING 11.11 The CSS for pinch to zoom

```css
body {
    margin:0;
    padding:0;
    background: #fff;
    height:2000px;
    width: 100%;
}

#holder {
    margin:0;
    padding:0;
    position: absolute;
    box-sizing: border-box;
    top:0;
    left:0;
    overflow: hidden;
    background: #fff;
    border: 5px solid green;
    bottom:0;
    right:0;
}

#img {
    -webkit-transform-origin: 0 0;
    transform-origin: 0 0;
    position: absolute;
    background: url('images/chicken_q.jpg');
    background-size: 100%;
    display: block;
    background-repeat: no-repeat;
    height: 200px;
    width: 300px;
}
```

INITIALIZING AND CORRECTING THE LAYOUT

The first thing the JavaScript needs to do is hide the address bar. Doing that is as simple as calling `window.scrollTo(0,1)`. Calling this immediately will not work in iOS because at initial page load the browser has no height.

A 50 ms timeout solves this problem with a barely perceptible delay. Then the #holder element needs to be fit to the screen. Another timeout is required so the correct screen value is available when the scroll that hides the address bar finishes. Finally the rebuild function is subscribed to the orientation change event so the whole operation can be performed again if the user rotates her device (**Listing 11.12**).

LISTING 11.12 Initializing the layout

```
function rebuild(){

    setTimeout(function(){

        var box;
        //detect the size of the viewable area,
        //hchrome and vchrome are the area lost to OS chrome,
        //based on browser detection
        if(Math.abs(window.orientation) > 0 ) {
            box = [screen.height, screen.width - hchrome];
        } else {
            box = [screen.width, screen.height - vchrome];
        }

        $('#holder').style.height = box[1] + 'px';
        $('#holder').style.width = box[0] + 'px';
        hero.fitToBox(box);
        window.scrollTo(0,1);

    }, 50);
}


window.setTimeout(function(){
    window.scrollTo(0,1);
    rebuild();
}, 50);


document.addEventListener('orientationchange', rebuild);
```

This example doesn't show how to determine what to subtract to account for browser chrome, but the full code is available in Listing 11.17 on the book's website.

You'll notice the hero object in the rebuild function. This is a singleton function that encapsulates the behavior of the scaled object. The fitToBox method positions the image in the viewport (**Listing 11.13**).

LISTING 11.13 Creating the hero object

```
//hardcoded values from the large size of the
//chicken image
var imageHeight = 1267;
var imageWidth = 1900;

function $(selector) {
   return document.querySelector(selector);
}

var hero = (function(init){

   var currentDims = [], top = 0, left = 0, center = [0,0]

   image = $('#img');

   setSrc('images/chicken_s.jpg');


   //set a new src, waits until the new image is loaded before replacing it
   function setSrc(src) {
      var img = new Image();
      img.onload = function(){
         console.log('loaded ' + src);
         image.style.backgroundImage = 'url('+ src+ ')';
      }
      img.src = src;
   }

   function setScale(scale, animate) {
      /* See Listing 11.15 */
   }
```

```
function fitToBox(dimsArr) {
    var imgw, imgh, scaleFactor;
    var w = dimsArr[0], h = dimsArr[1];

    //this is a landscape photo so I can assume w > h
    imgw = w;

    scaleFactor = w/imageWidth;
    imgh = Math.round(imageHeight * scaleFactor);
    image.style.width = imgw  +'px';
    image.style.height = imgh + 'px';
    currentDims = [imgw, imgh];
    top = (h/2) - (imgh/2);
    image.style.top = top + 'px';

}

function setCenter(centerArr) {
    center = centerArr;
}

return {

    setScale: setScale,
    setCenter: setCenter,
    fitToBox: fitToBox,
    setSrc:setSrc
}
}());
```

To center the image, find the center of the viewport (the height divided by two). Then subtract half the height of the element, aligning it with the center. Store this position as top for use later.

PREVENTING SCROLLING

Before handling touch events, we need to do one more piece of housekeeping. Zooming is disabled in the viewport meta property, but scrolling is not. Scrolling will also interfere with the pinch gesture.

To disable it you must `preventDefault` on all touch events. The only way to do this reliably is to assign a function to the `ontouchmove` member of the document object. `addEventListener` will not work in this case:

```
document.ontouchmove = function(e){
    e.preventDefault();
}
```

HANDLING TOUCHES

To scale the element we need to do two things: find the center of the two touches to define the point we're going to scale from, then determine a scaling factor from the pinch gesture.

Finding the center point

Safari actually provides the center point of the touchpoints on the touch event object (`event.pageX` and `event.pageY`). That's useful, but don't bother with it because this information is not provided by any other browser. Instead, you can easily derive the center point from the positions of the other two touchpoints. The center point is the average of the two points:

```
var x = (e.touches[0].pageX + e.touches[1].pageX)/2;
var y = (e.touches[0].pageY + e.touches[1].pageY)/2;
```

This approach works in Safari, Firefox, and multi-touch aware Android browsers.

Determining a scaling factor

Safari provides a `scale` property on the `Event` object that gives you the value you want right away, but other browsers don't, so we'll calculate the scale factor. The scale factor is the current distance between the touchpoints divided by the starting distance. Determining the distance between two points uses a modification of the Pythagorean theorem, called the distance formula. Given points A and B, distance d is defined by the following formula:

$$d = \sqrt{(x_A \; x_B)^2 + (y_A \; y_B)^2}$$

The code is shown in **Listing 11.14**.

LISTING 11.14 Using the distance formula

```
function dist(pointA, pointB) {
    return Math.sqrt(
        Math.pow((pointA[0] - pointB[0]),2) +
        Math.pow((pointA[1] - pointB[1]),2)
    );
}
```

Next, we'll create a single function to handle all touch events (**Listing 11.15**). Because the hero object has methods that take a scale factor and a center point, we'll determine those inside the touch handler, before passing them to the relevant methods of the hero object.

LISTING 11.15 Handling all touch events

```
var startLen;

function handleTouch(e) {

    e.preventDefault;

    var x,y,len;

    if(e.type == 'touchstart') {
        //update the src for higher quality zooming
        hero.setSrc('images/chicken_l.jpg');

        if(e.touches.length > 1) {

        startLen = dist(
            [e.touches[0].screenX, e.touches[0].screenY],
            [e.touches[1].screenX, e.touches[1].screenY]
        );

        }

    } else if(e.type == 'touchmove' && e.touches.length == 2) {

        x = (e.touches[0].pageX + e.touches[1].pageX)/2;
        y = (e.touches[0].pageY + e.touches[1].pageY)/2;

        hero.setCenter([Math.round(x),Math.round(y)]);


        len = dist(
            [e.touches[0].screenX,e.touches[0].screenY],
            [e.touches[1].screenX, e.touches[1].screenY]
        );


        hero.setScale(len/startLen);
```

```
    } else if (e.type == 'touchend' || e.type == 'touchcancel'){

        hero.setScale(1, true);

    }
}
```

SCALING THE ELEMENT

Scaling in CSS is proportional around the transform-origin. Because proportional scaling is built into CSS we need only worry about one vertex: the top left. The rest of the vertices will take care of themselves as you scale the object.

The only thing that's a little tricky here is that for performance reasons we'll want to apply the scale with CSS transforms, which are calculated based on an object's local coordinates, but the touchpoint positions are relative to the top left of the browser.

It's not possible to query the DOM and determine the size of the transformed element (transforms are applied after CSS positioning), so we'll need to do some arithmetic to determine the correct values (**Listing 11.16**).

LISTING 11.16 Applying the transformation

```
function setScale(scale, animate) {
    //this is to allow animated "snap back behavior"
    if(animate) {
        image.style[TRANSITION] = TRANSFORM_CSS + ' 0.2s ease-out';
    } else {
        image.style[TRANSITION] = 'none';
    }

    //center is the previously set center point of the transform
    var tx = center[0] + scale * (0 - center[0]);
    var ty = center[1] + scale * (top - center[1]);

    //turn page coordinate into an object coordinate.
    //this does not need to be done for X because the image is flush with the
    //side of the browser
    ty = ty - top;
    image.style[TRANSFORM] =
        'matrix(' + scale+ ',0,0,' + scale + ',' + tx + ',' + ty +')';

}
```

This complete example results in an element that scales with your fingers properly and snaps back to its original scale at the end of the gesture.

PINCHING NEXT STEPS

This is just the beginning of what you can do with complex gestures. The pinch example described here has one key feature: the target of the gesture always moves while the user's fingers are moving. If you want the image to snap to a certain scale rather than stop the movement at that time, wait until the end of the gestures to determine if a threshold has been crossed.

NOTE: The complete listing, including the following snippet, can be found on the website in Listing 11.17.

```
} else if(e.type == 'touchmove' && e.touches.length == 2) {

  /** snip **/

    //a variable inside the parent scope.
    lastScale = len/startLen;

  hero.setScale(len/startLen);


} else if (e.type == 'touchend' || e.type == 'touchcancel'){

  if(lastScale < 1.5) {
    hero.setScale(1, true); //with animation
  } else {
    hero.setScale(2, true);
  }
```

This ensures that the user always has feedback and never feels like the interface has stopped responding. The smooth animation also shows the user what happened, rather than giving the impression of a jump or stutter.

When building this example you might have noticed that the image, when scaled, became blurry. That's because, as discussed in Chapter 7, "CSS Transitions, Animation, and Transforms," the element was rendered before being handed to the GPU. To remove the blur simply convert the 3D transform to a 2D transform.

WRAPPING UP

This chapter introduced you to multi-touch gestures. You learned how to detect multiple touches in WebKit and Mozilla touch events and in Microsoft's pointer events. Many gestures are complicated and at the moment you'll need a fair amount of geometry to be successful. The great thing about geometry is that it works and understanding the math allows you to do the calculations purely in JavaScript, without talking to the DOM.

This is also the end of this book. Hopefully you are now in a good position to start building your own HTML5 touch interfaces. Things are changing very quickly on the mobile web, but one thing is clear: the mobile web will continue to grow and future mobile devices will have touch interfaces.

PROJECT

In the project in the previous chapter, you built a swipeable image gallery. Now take the same gallery and add a zoom feature. When the user double taps (two taps within 100 ms of each other) on the image, it should zoom to its largest possible size. The zoom should be animated and the swiping behavior should not break.

Then make it so a user can also "unpinch" on the photo to enlarge it. The photo should snap to either the largest possible size or its original size.

INDEX

NUMBERS